WINNING GROUP SALES PRESENTATIONS: A GUIDE TO CLOSING THE DEAL

WINNING GROUP SALES PRESENTATIONS: A GUIDE TO CLOSING THE DEAL

LINDA RICHARDSON

McGraw-Hill
New York   San Francisco   Washington, D.C.   Auckland   Bogotá
Caracas   Lisbon   London   Madrid   Mexico City   Milan
Montreal   New Delhi   San Juan   Singapore
Sydney   Tokyo   Toronto

McGraw-Hill

A Division of The **McGraw·Hill** Companies

Library of Congress Cataloging-in-Publication Data

Richardson, Linda
    Winning group sales presentations: a guide to closing the deal /
Linda Richardson.
        p.   cm.
    Includes index.
    ISBN 1-55623-259-4   ISBN 1-55623-297-7 (Special edition)
    ISBN 1-55623-690-5 (Paperback edition)
    1. Sales presentations.   I.   Title.
    HF5438.8.P74R43   1990
    658.8'101 — dc20   89–33224
                                                                         CIP

Printed in the United States of America
9 10 DOC/DOC 0 9 8 7 6 5 4 3 2 1 0

Just as we sell to groups and in groups,
so too inspiration is collective.

For sharing your friendship and gifts—
my thanks to:
Ian Woodner, Ed Cohen, Alexandra Reed Lajoux,
Megan Cook, Bill Gerich, Tranda Fischelis,
Terry MacColl Charlton, Bridget Palmer, George Bruns, and
D. J. O'Loughlin.

FOREWORD

Linda Richardson has done an incredible favor for all of us in the sales field: she's created an easy-to-learn and simple-to-use process for dealing with the group selling situation, and the timing couldn't have been better. First, the phrase *global competition* is striking fear in the hearts of most U.S. corporations. The bottom line of the new game is that more sellers are chasing relatively fewer buyers. We're discovering as never before that there's a finite number of customers out there. Every day more sellers are giving these customers more options, more opportunities, and more ways of forming new and different buying relationships. And, unfortunately, many of these are *our* customers.

Today, being *good* barely gets you off the bench and into the game. For those who would like to call themselves professionals, getting better is what it's about. This means continuous improvement, continuous learning, and continuous growth. This growth has to be in step with the way the world and the marketplace are going. There are new trends occurring in this fast-paced world of industrial buying and selling. The first trend involves "multiple buying influences." The old selling picture showed buyer and seller sitting across the desk from one another as though they were the only actors playing in the drama. In the industrial sales world that was never an accurate picture of the actual sales process; today, it would be a total distortion. What is more common today for major buying decisions is a group sell, with a buying team sitting across from a salesperson or a selling team. It's a new game with different rules to obey and different skills to master. And, more often that not, we're talking about a big-ticket sale. It's not just the sale we can't afford to lose—it's the customer.

All of this is good news for those salespeople willing to be a learning participant with Linda Richardson in this book.What makes it especially good news is that everything you ever wanted to know about group selling is included. This is an easy-to-read, how-to process. It's like attending a seminar or, better yet, having a series of one-on-one counseling sessions with a true expert who has been there and done our homework for us, with great attention to both the big picture as well as to the all-important details.

The fact is, I was both embarrassed and excited as I read what Linda wrote about the group sale. I was embarrassed to discover that recently I had missed applying some of the most key and basic ideas. Yet I was also excited to realize how easily I can reeducate myself to remember to include what I've been missing. Linda covers it all, from building credibility and trust to dealing with late-comers to a meeting; from differentiating your product to how to put on a full-blown client conference.

Winning Group Sales Presentations: A Guide to Closing the Deal is more than a book—it's a tool kit for the sales professional. My advice to you, the reader, is to open this kit, pick out each tool carefully, master its use, and let it become a servant to you.Use these tools to leverage your own *continuous improvement* and your own *continuous success* as a sales professional. Linda has done the hard work for us all. It's a gift from a true professional to those who want to become more professional. Enjoy!

Larry Wilson
Chairman and Chief Executive Officer
Pecos River Learning Centers, Inc.

CONTENTS

INTRODUCTION

A revolution has taken place in the way big-ticket buyers make buying decisions. When it comes to making a big-ticket sale or a sale that will affect several departments in your client's organization, rarely today at the final stages will you be selling to *one* buyer, regardless of your product, service, idea, or industry. And although your big ticket sale may begin one-on-one, chances are you will be closing with a *group* of decision-makers—as few as two or as many as thirty.

More and more organizations are transferring the responsibility for making buying decisions from individuals to groups. And more and more often you will be one of several groups competing in what has been labeled a "beauty pageant." Judged on the how and who as much as on the what, these contests are among the most intense forms of business competition. Even when there are only one or two key decision-makers in the group, their response to you will be shaped by how you deal with all the players.

Why this trend toward selling to client groups? The roots of selling to a group run deep and broad. The philosophy of group participation as a way to improve the quality of decisions has been making its way to the buying table for decades, sped by a growing determination to reduce the risk associated with big ticket decisions, and an increasing need to get "buy in" from the people who will make the decision "happen" once it is made.

The need to sell to multiple buyers has altered the rules of selling: how today's salespeople sell, to whom they sell, how long they sell, and *what* they sell. Today's salesperson no longer functions as the Lone Ranger, but as part of a sales team that includes specialists, as well as generalists, and seniors as well as associates. The intense competition has created a "client generation" made up of demanding and sophisticated clients. Even relationship-oriented clients, feeling the pressure to get the best deal, are "shopping" to make sure they get it. All this has lengthened the sales cycle. To add to the challenges, clients and salespeople alike say they find it difficult to differentiate between look-alike products.

Amid these changes, however, the basic *purpose* of selling remains constant. All clients still have unmet objectives and they are all still looking for ways to achieve them. The task at hand is *how* to sell in our *new* environment—the era of selling to client groups.

To exploit this group selling revolution, salespeople need to recraft their one-on-one selling skills. Although group selling skills do not replace one-on-one skills, they do build on them. Group selling skills offer a second tier of one-on-one skills to equip salespeople to cope with the many differences indigenous to selling to a group, from satisfying multiple client needs all at once, to the pressures of being "on stage" before a group.

I know firsthand how different one-on-one selling and selling to a group can be. I've been there! More than ten years ago, when I made my first sales presentation to a client group, I knew intuitively that group selling was different from one-on-one selling, but I didn't know what to do about the difference. Although I had been confident and successful in one-on-one, one-on-two, and two-on-two selling situations, the minute I found myself facing the group of eight senior clients, I felt my heart pound and heard my voice quiver—why? This was new territory. The big-ticket item I was selling involved several key departments in the client organization, and the senior manager of each one was there to evaluate me so that the group could make a decision. Eight pairs of eyes were staring at me. All were waiting for me to present something on which they would base a yea or nay vote later—*after I was gone.*

Who should I focus on? Could I establish rapport with the group? Probe for needs? Get involvement? My gut reaction (fear) said *no way*, so I abandoned my interactive one-on-one selling skills and proceeded with a monologue presentation. What else can you do with a group, I asked myself, but no other answer came. I knew then that something different was going on, but I didn't know what.

We did get the contract, despite my poor group sale. In those days my company had almost no competition and in retrospect I can see that we didn't win votes during the group sell but *after* it, when I was able to get back to each member individually or through correspondence. I never actually "sold the group." I never really lit a fire under them—how could I when I positioned myself as a speaker—speaking *at*, not *with*, the group.

Since that first timorous monologue, I have made several hundred sales presentations to client decision-making groups, sometimes alone and sometimes with a team from my training company. Like my clients, I still call *group selling* a presentation, but I now know that group selling is very different from a speech-like presentation in *two* important ways. First, its objective is to sell, and second, it demands more interaction with the group. At my company, our group selling success ratio now runs a high 9 out of 10. To achieve that record, we have built up skills by trial, error, and inspiration, participating in or observing hundreds of presentations. More importantly, we learned from teaching these skills to more than one thousand bankers, investment bankers, product specialists and professionals from almost every other industry.

I now know by experience what I knew that first day by instinct: the one-on-one selling approach needs to be tempered when selling to a group. Group selling and one-on-one selling are different and the gap between them, while small, is wide enough to make the difference between winning and losing. Since most competitors also have good people and good products, the difference that the client ultimately perceives is created by the presenter. Today, I know how to take advantage of this.

Selling one-on-one and selling to a group are as different as a game of catch is from juggling. Hand-eye coordination is needed for both, but the juggler must coordinate many objects— not just one—all the while still satisfying audience expectations. As a salesperson, you already know how to "play catch." The question is, can you juggle?

Sales calls usually occur between one or two salespersons and one client. But a sales call is transformed into group selling when a group of clients (2 to 30 or more) are present. Selling to several clients at one time changes the chemistry and reality of the situation.

- The salesperson or sales team is *more* visible, while the *needs* of the clients are *less* visible and more numerous.
- Presenters are "looked over" while their message may be overlooked.
- Clients let salespeople talk, talk, talk their way right out of a sale.

And that's only the beginning. Group selling is truly a sales revolution—one that calls for you to use your one-on-one skills in a new way. This book will show you how to structure and deliver a top-notch presentation, how to prepare and organize your team, and how to develop and organize your materials. It will help you build and refine your one-on-one selling skills and become more comfortable and effective when selling to client groups.

Most importantly, this book will help you to become more aware of *how* you present . . . enabling you to see yourself as the others see you (and believe me, they *are* looking!). The following pages will help you handle presentations from development to delivery, starting with the selling basics.

Here's the checklist:

- *The whos*—Who will be at the sales presentation from the client's side? Who will *not* be there? Who is the powerful client decision-maker and who are influencers? What are the political sensitivities of the mix of people in the room? Who, if anyone, should you include from your organization? Who and how many should be a part of your team?
- *The whats*—What is your strategy? What should you present? What should you include in your proposal? Exclude? In what order should you make your points? What addenda does the proposal need? What handouts or materials will you need? What equipment will you need?
- *The whens*—When should you present? Should you be first/last in the procession of competitors? What time slot should you

take? When should you distribute your proposal? Should you send it in advance? When should you use your visual aids and handout materials?

• *The wheres*—Where is the best place to present? Where will the clients be seated? Where will you be? Where will you sit or stand in relation to the key decision-maker(s)? How will the room be set up? How do you want the room set up?

• *The hows*—How should you prepare? How do you get participation from the group? How can you maintain control? How do you deal with different levels of interest and support? How do you communicate with several clients at one time, addressing each client's individual concerns while keeping the group intact? How should you divide your attention? How can you project confidence, minimize nervousness, and control stage fright? How do you motivate the group to take action? How do you maximize your team?

Of course, not every selling situation requires that you sell to a group. Some buy decisions are still made by one buyer based on one-on-one sales calls without a presentation to a team of decision-makers. But when clients use buying committees, you had better know who, what, where, when and how—or someone else will walk away with the business.

When you find yourself selling to a group, the situations will most likely either be a "foot in the door," "a proforma," or a "last chance." "Foot in the door" sales situations arise when clients require you to make an introductory capabilities presentation to a committee before you can even qualify to compete. Market research firms, for example, usually have to be on approved lists to get in the running. On the other end of the spectrum, you might be in the enviable position of giving a final proforma verification—you may no longer be in any real competition with anyone, as the client has all but selected you, contingent on your presentation.

But *most* typically you will be giving your sales presentation as a "last chance"—ideally to be the winner—in what salespeople and clients call the "beauty pageant."

The contest can be grueling for both clients and contenders. In this tough and highly competitive environment, salespeople can be given as little as 20 minutes and as long as three hours.

One firm over a one-week period called in 26 banks before it selected one. In another case, a single day was reserved for five sales presentations. Over an eight-hour period, a team of nine client decision-makers reviewed a procession of sales presentations back-to-back, and by 6:30 p.m. they had made their choice. In both cases, while all of the competitors had spent a substantial amount of time and money up to that point, and all had good people and good products, only one firm walked out with the deal. Except for rare co-management opportunities, there is no "place and show." There is only "win."

Group selling is not easy. The life-or-death "survival" nature of group selling, the challenges of group "size," starting with the high level of client expectation, nervousness, top competitors, and more—all make group selling more challenging than the one-on-one selling. One client is not likely to "hold court," so to speak. But when several clients convene to pass collective judgement, needs and agendas multiply, egos emerge, the pressure builds, expectations rise, and all eyes turn to you.

Now, let's look at how to win in this environment by considering structure, delivery, preparation, and packaging.

STRUCTURE—THE GROUP SELLING FRAMEWORK

INTRODUCING THE FRAMEWORK

Have you ever wished you had help in organizing your presentation to a client group? Many top salespeople readily admit that it's hard to know how to start—what to include and where to include it. Fortunately, there is a simple and practical framework that you can use to develop and deliver your presentation.

When a group of clients is present, you will need to "orchestrate"—and the more clients, the more orchestration. The group selling framework will help you with this orchestration and achieve an element of spontaneity, too. There are eight distinct phases in an effective group sales presentation. Understanding and using them will able you to organize your ideas and maximize your time. The phases are:

- *Opening*
- *Agenda*
- *Client Needs Check*
- *Body of Presentation*
- *Summary*
- *Q&A*
- *Close*
- *Follow-Up*

At first glance, these phases may look obvious, but most salespeople neglect at least one of them. As the number of clients increases, the need for a framework also increases. With one client you can skip around and still remain cohesive. But to keep a client group on track you will need to present your material logically, using transitions like, "Let's move on . . .," "There are three main points," or "There are advantages and disadvantages."

Before looking at each of the eight elements in depth, it is important to look at the underlying premise that governs the sales presentation framework especially in today's environment: *the more "give-and-take" there is throughout your sales presentation, the greater the likelihood of your winning the business.* Because at least one of your competitors at the presentation stage is likely to have people and products equally matched to yours, differentiation is one of your major challenges. Being able to create give-and-take will help you to meet this challenge. In the past the product was a key differentiator; but today, because products look alike, differentiation often lies in factors *outside* the product—understanding and relating to the client's needs, winning the client's trust, and building credibility. These factors are developed in "give-and-take" between you and your clients.

Most salespeople involved in group selling sense that it is different from selling one-on-one, but instead of *building* on their one-on-one skills, they *abandon* them and *lecture* at the client. In one-on-one selling, by the very nature of the situation, give-and-take can occur more naturally. Unfortunately, most salespeople approach selling to a group as if it were a speech. They present their product/idea from A to Z, rattling off points in sequence while the clients (hopefully) listen, and then they open the discussion to a Q&A.

This A to Z approach shuts out client input, discourages client questions, and most importantly ignores the client's sequence. A to Z places the full burden on the product and the salesperson's "getting it right." It also creates a situation in which the salesperson walks out of the presentation with little or no idea of what the client thinks of his or her presentation. It is a rare salesperson who doesn't report being more nervous during the "A to Z" monologue and much more comfortable during an interaction of Q&A. They say in the "give-and-take" of the Q&A they feel more natural and spontaneous. So why not build this into the entire presentation?

In the 1960s and early 1970s, the A to Z followed by Q&A approach was more effective, primarily because there were fewer competitors, greater differences among products, and clients who were less demanding, less knowledgeable, and less sophisticated. But today the old model of A to Z followed by Q&A can result in undistinguishable and undistinguished presentations that leave "insider" clients out in the cold. In an A to Z presentation, the spotlight is on you as the salesperson and your product or idea. Today, however, you need to *share* the spotlight with your clients. With a few small shifts in the A to Z approach, you can differentiate your presentation and inject it with client synergy. Now let's look in depth at the phases of the group selling framework and how to make them work for you.

THE OPENING

INTRODUCTION

One senior manager in a prestigious international consulting firm still recalls how his heart pounded when he had to address the board of a leading company for the first time. He introduced himself and his team members and then told the group why the subject of this address was so timely and important. As he spoke, he read interest in the clients' eyes and "just took it from there." He did a *few small things right,* and this enabled him to get off to an excellent start. This chapter is about getting those "few small things" right.

In the first few minutes of the presentation, clients form a general impression of you. During that time they may be so absorbed in trying to "place" you that they may not listen to precisely what you are saying. But by understanding what the opening is really about, you can make yours more effective. The opening is not the end-all and be-all as often mistakenly thought but an important piece of your total picture. For an effective opening, you need to:

- *Establish rapport*
- *Begin to build your credibility*
- *Tell clients who you are—introduce yourself/your team/ your organization*
- *Thank clients for the opportunity to present*
- *Gain client interest as you present your objective (why you are there)*
- *Increase client interest as you discuss your purpose (why it is worthwhile for client to be there)*

These opening tasks might seem too much to handle, especially in the midst of presenter's "stage fright," but mastering how to open will reduce the anxiety often felt in the opening. Granted, the prospect of facing several near strangers—or even clients you know—as a group can make you nervous.

Unfortunately many salespeople fail to do "a few small things right" and pay dearly for it. Being nervous before a group or clients is natural, even desirable. Like the athlete's adrenaline, it can push you towards peak performance. But nervousness without know-how will get you nowhere, and adlibbing is no way out. If you know how to open, you will find the natural confidence that can get you off to a winning start. So let's look at *how* to open effectively, starting from your *first* opening—your arrival at your presentation.

ARRIVAL OPENING

There are really two openings in a sales presentation: your *arrival opening* (walking in, saying hello, shaking hands), and then the *more formal opening* with the group.

The arrival opening is a "godsend." During arrival openings you have an opportunity for *one-on-one contact* and the natural rapport it engenders. It can help you feel more comfortable. The arrival opening offers other advantages, as one salesperson found out the hard way. While common sense would have dictated that he arrive at least 20 minutes before his presentation, he allowed himself only five minutes before he was to begin. He spent his pre-presentation time organizing his materials, pausing to give a quick hello to his contact and the other four deciders.

His papers were perfect but his presentation failed. Why? By concentrating on his own handwriting he missed the "writing on the wall." Not only did he fail to use the arrival opening to "reach out and touch," he also failed to learn that one of the seniors in the group, the one who championed his idea, had resigned earlier in the day. He was told this vital piece of information *after* his presentation. Partly because he had not broken the ice with the group, and partly because they were distracted by the high-level resignation, he and the group never clicked. Worst of all, he positioned most of his presentation to the senior who was on his way out! He was not even invited back to present again after the dust settled.

Even if you don't get hot-off-the-press news, arriving early will often give you access to other helpful information. A consultant who arrived at 12:30 for his 1:00 presentation was invited to have a "quick sandwich" with the group he would be presenting to. During the lunch the group spoke openly about the competitor who had just presented—what they liked and what they didn't like. With this information the consultant was able to position his ideas to their thinking. Another salesperson arrived at 1:50 for his 2:30 presentation to see a key competitor leaving 10 minutes early from his one-hour presentation, looking flushed and unhappy. Since the salesperson had been worried sick about this very competitor, this glimpse was the little push he needed to inspire him to make a winning presentation.

Aside from giving you early warning of calamities or inside news, arriving early enough *before* clients get there will enable you to organize the room to your advantage to maximize the setting. Before the clients arrive, if possible, size up the room and when necessary move extra chairs to avoid "black holes" that impede communication, particularly the two seats to the right and left of you that invariably are left empty and will separate you symbolically as well as physically from clients in the group.

Arriving early will help you *start on time*. Being late in a sales situation is always bad, but it is worse when selling to a group. I know of one sales team that arrived 40 minutes late for its presentation to a Fortune 500 company because of flight delays. They were asked to cool their heels while a competitor took their time slot. Senior managers, obviously annoyed after waiting 15 minutes, had ushered in another sales team that happened to have arrived two hours early because of flights. While any one member of the client team would probably have been more understanding in a one-on-one situation, the group members' intolerance increased geometrically as they waited *together* in the conference room away from their desks. The team that arrived late did get a chance to tell their story, but when they did they were flustered and apologetic. The intrinsic "chill factor" of the group setting did little to put the presenters at ease. Two weeks later they learned that they lost out. Their lateness might not have been the final blow, but it certainly did not advance their cause.

Most importantly, an early arrival enables you to make that all-important *individual* personal contact, saying hello and shaking hands with people as they come in so you can establish rapport. If you do not know some of the group members, ask your contact to introduce you. If there is *no one* to *introduce you, don't be shy; get up and introduce yourself.* Work the room! Even if there are 25 people present, get up, and move around and introduce yourself to each one. Someone who makes it difficult for you to introduce yourself by looking away or appearing preoccupied may be signaling to you that he or she is not a supporter— especially if this person takes the chair furthest from you. To counteract such resistance, *be sure to make eye contact with this person* and include him or her during your presentation. Whatever you do, do not ignore this person.

FORMAL OPENING

Introductions

Be sure not to skip the formal opening of your presentation. Although you may have said hello and socialized during the arrival phase, you need the opening to "pull the group together" and to address them as a group.

It is in this initial opening segment that many presenters have bouts with nervousness. While it is true that your opening sets the tone, it is *not* the most important part of your presentation. Far more important is the sum total of what will follow. Many professionals confuse selling with making a speech, where the opening *is* disproportionately important. The exact words are far less important than the level of comfort and confidence that you project. The nervous tension often associated with opening with a group can be attributed in part to this overemphasis, but it also results from not knowing how to open.

Some people can—thanks to natural-born talent, experience, and or training—find it easy to make excellent, strong "front-door" openings. But *every salesperson* who can sell one-on-one can make at least a *very good* "side entrance" opening with a group. It may not be as strong, but it can be effective enough to keep the group with them until their full strength can come through during the presentation.

Remember, the opening is only one important piece of your presentation, not the only important part. Your opening needs to be confident, but it cannot carry you. It is throughout your presentation that you will need to win over your clients by involving them, addressing their needs, and persuading them that *you* are the one to best meet their needs.

Nervous Jitters

To reduce nervousness in the opening, the best thing you can do is to keep the opening in its proper perspective and be as natural as possible. Of course, this is easy to say, but it can be done if you do a few small things. Personally, I have found a way to help me be natural regardless how nervous I am. I do exactly what I do on one-on-one calls even if there are ten or more clients. As I start, I look at *one* person as I begin. This brings out my one-on-one self and my one-on-one comfort level. By *looking* at someone and speaking to him or her for up to three seconds and then looking at someone else, you too can "force" your one-on-one self to emerge. Most openings sound stilted, but by using your eyes you can infuse your voice with life and make your "thank you's," introductions, and opening comments more genuine. Instead of looking at one person, most salespeople, because they are nervous or don't know an alternative, look at a blurred sea of faces or at the back wall—even tabletops or the floor. This only hinders communication. Group protocol allows you about *three* to *five* seconds (faster will make you seem jumpy) of eye contact with each person. Before you begin, if the group is large (15 to 30 or so), you can section off the group into segments of four people or so. Especially as the group size increases, as you look at one person in each segment, the colleagues sitting to the right or left of him or her will feel as if you are looking at them.

As you look at each client, do not go around the table Pac-Man fashion (digesting each one in order), but look at individuals naturally in a random fashion, turning toward them gently as you speak.

Not only will looking at individuals help you sound and feel natural, it will also help you take the focus and the pressure off yourself as you connect with and read the group. *As simple as this technique is, it is the last thing many salespeople think of.* Good one-on-one salespeople often say they are not themselves— not as effective— when they present to a group. Little wonder, since they fail to do the very things that would come so naturally one-on-one, such as using their eyes to help communicate their message and "read" what is going on. (Please see "Eye Contact," Page 95 and "Presence/Nervousness," Page 77/80.)

Introducing Yourself, Your Team Members, Your Organization

Your introductions should be concise. Be genuine and friendly to help establish rapport and credibility but keep your introductions short. And if you are less experienced, *rehearse* (don't memorize word for word) what you will say about yourself, your team members, and your organization. (Please see "Team," Page 143.)

Once you introduce yourself and your role, if you are a part of a team, introduce your team members. Neglecting to introduce your team members or doing so half-heartedly is not only discourteous—it hurts the sale!

As you introduce yourself, state your name (unless you have been introduced by the client) and your role *as it relates to the client and the situation at hand.* If you are leading the team, introduce your team members, but do not go into detail at this point. Briefly state their roles in the presentation and personalize each introduction as much as possible to help build the credibility of your *team.* Help your clients "translate" the trust they have in you into trust in your team. For example, you might say, "Bill, our specialist . . . and I have worked together . . . his attention to detail and grasp of clients' needs. . . ." Of course, if you know every person in the room and are sure they know you and your team, common sense should prevail, and you should forgo introductions.

Plan what you will say about your organization, emphasizing what is relevant to your client. For example, for a privately held traditional client you might mention your long history. *Remember clients are more interested in the kind of deals/business you have done relevant to their situation than in general information about your organization.* How much your client knows about you and your organization will also help determine how much information you provide and how you position your organization. For example, a firm that is a household word in New York can be almost unknown in the West or with middle market companies. In a sale in those markets, the team must establish its credibility without conveying "New York" slickness. They may need to swallow their big time pride as they present their track record so they don't appear arrogant. Also once you present a feature to describe your organization, draw the conclusion for the clients so that they can see the benefit to them of that feature. A salesperson who didn't do that never got full mileage out of his company's ownership of a leading automotive magazine. He left it to his automotive client to deduce what this meant: he had immediate access to the top experts in the field. As you introduce your organization, highlight key clients that your prospect knows (same industry, area) and admires (profitable leaders in industry). One consultant unfortunately turned off his prospect group by citing some of the largest multinationals in the world as his clients. Unfortunately his middle market prospect could not relate to his client base. The reason the client gave for selecting a competitor: "We didn't think you would understand our market."

Thank You's

Your thank you's can come before or after you have made your introductions. A simple, genuine comment like (as you are looking at someone), "We would like to thank you for your consideration of our proposal . . ." will let your clients know you appreciate being there and respect their time and attention. Use your introduction to begin personalizing your presentation for the client. For example, if you know someone in the group and it is appropriate, use his/her name—"John pioneered this concept two years ago. . . ." Keep the compliments in check or you may sound obsequious.

Summary of Events That Lead to the Sale Presentation

Once the introduction and thank yous are completed, you should give a very *brief* summary of the events that have led up to your presentation. For example: you might say, "I have met with Bob . . . We (*brief summary statement of what transpired to get you to this stage*) . . ." Be sure to give credit to clients such as Bob who have helped you up to this point and thank them for their help. Whatever you do, don't overdo the historical background or you will put everyone to sleep. One salesperson used to spend about one-third of his time giving background. His results were as blah as his presentation. Today he limits his summary to about four minutes at most. If you wish to achieve a more dramatic effect you can hold this information until after you state your objective and purpose.

What's in It for the Client—Objective & Purpose

Now you are ready for the all-important task of giving the client a reason to listen to you. This is where you present your objective and purpose, two sides of the same coin. The objective is what you want to cover and the purpose is what the client will derive from listening to you—why you are there and what's in it for the client. *If possible, avoid the trite beginning, "Today (this morning/afternoon/evening), I would like to talk about. . . ."* This overused opening rarely conveys the heart of why you are there. It usually sounds wooden and often fails to capture the clients' attention. You want your opening to tell the client group *very early on* what they want to know—*"What's in it for US?"*

One operations manager learned this on the firing line of an internal sale. He opened with "plastic" words and an artificial tone to match, saying, "I am here this morning to present to you a system for introducing a new product, to tell you about my department's role in this process, and tell you how we can save you time." His colleagues were not exactly on the edge of their seats. A senior salesperson interrupted and challenged him by asking, "Why should we listen to you talk about your role in introducing a new product?" The seemingly tough guy was really expressing what every client is silently asking as you open—"What's in it for me?" The salesperson thought for a moment. He *looked* at the salesperson and then, in an *animated, natural* voice, he captured in three hard-hitting sentences what he wanted to say: "Corporate Finance is always creating new products, but because the support departments such as legal and accounting that should be in to the loop are not brought in in the early stages, too many of the new products *blow up* when they hit the system. And everybody, *revenue and operations,* gets frustrated. *We* can help make sure that doesn't happen." He had discovered his natural opening. He was far more engaging and animated. He was more relaxed. He allowed his commitment to show through. He had answered the all-important question: "What's in it for the client?" The group was all ears. *All presenters who believe in what they are talking about have a natural opening inside of them.* They simply have to find it.

Finding Your Natural Opening

Preparation (but not word-for-word memorization) is usually needed to find your natural opening. Unfortunately, these usually don't pop out naturally. My college writing teacher use to say, "To write, just begin. Then cross out your first sentence." She understood that many of us get off to a slow, stilted start—that trying to start can actually block creativity. This "cross-out technique" can help you say what you really want to say as you prepare your presentation. A good exercise to help you develop your natural opening is to write out what might be a typically trite "Today. . ." opening, and then play devil's advocate to yourself by asking, *"Why* should they listen to that?" As you answer this question, you will probably find your "natural" opening, the one that gets to the fundamental reason why you are there and what value you can bring to the client.

Natural openings can use an experience, a situation, an example, a war story, an anecdote, or industry knowledge ("We are seeing . . . in. . . .") that captures clients' attention and drives home bottom-line reasons to listen. It is the difference between "Today I am going to talk about ____" and "Corporate Finance is always creating new products. . . that blow up. . . ." Because your natural opening will be based on experience and real needs, it will come ready-made with your commitment and enthusiasm. Without these two elements, your opening (and your entire sales presentation) will fall flat. With these two elements, almost any opening can work.

While it helps to make the opening interesting and original, *it is more important to make it matter* and to make it natural and comfortable. Do not start with a brass band, *unless it is related* to the client's situation—and it may be. When the clients of a prominent architectural firm arrived to hear what could have been an everyday presentation, they saw a man in a gorilla costume crouched on a chair. The "gorilla" was more than theatrics. The lead salesperson began by introducing this team member, a nationally recognized authority on gorilla behavior who demonstrated—physically as well as conceptionally—critical aspects of their team's design for the gorilla facility at this major East Coast zoo. The design firm caught the clients' attention—and then satisfied their needs. Not surprisingly, they won the contract.

Personal experience and/or humor can sometimes engage a client's attention and interest in the opening. A researcher who was seeking a grant for a study on women entrepreneurship opened her presentation to a top women's group by saying, "I began my research for this presentation by going to the library. When I looked up 'women entrepreneurs' in the card catalogue, it said 'see men' " (pause). Spontaneous humor can also be effective. One timely joke saved a presenter from certain doom. He was the *fifth* panel member about to "rehash" *his* experience with Product X. He sensed the audience was getting edgy—and hungry since it was 12:30 p.m. He opened by repeating, "There were two spies—one Japanese, the other American—who were about to be shot. Each was granted a last wish. The Japanese asked to hear a tape extolling the superiority of Japanese management. The American asked to be shot first so that he wouldn't have to listen to it again!" "So," said the fifth speaker, "in the spirit of this noble sacrifice I would like to move directly to my summary points and then answer any questions you may have." The group appreciated both his humor and his sensitivity.

One sales presenter, banking on an excellent relationship with his client, opened with a daring visual approach. He flicked on his overhead projector. In large handwritten print on the screen appeared this plea:

*Please
Don't
Buy
Junk
Bonds*

He then proceeded to present an alternative tailor-made to fit his client's objectives. By the end of the presentation, they were convinced!

Another visual approach was taken by a speaker who addressed an audience of 150 bankers interested in marketing mutual funds. Although this was a speech and not a sales presentation, it taught a lot about the "show" aspect of a presentation. She opened by holding up a soiled rubber band, saying, "Many of you will recognize this item. It is a plain old rubber band." Audience members who were *not* looking at her—and at least half of them were not—raised their heads to look. She went on to tell them how she had called a major, well-respected mutual fund company on a Friday in August at 3:00 p.m. (a tough time for a salesperson to be "up") and had requested a particular prospectus. The salesman seemed annoyed by the call. His voice was flat. He was curt, short, disinterested. What she got in the mail were five prospectuses bound by a dirty rubber band. She then contrasted such "rubber-band marketing" to quality-service marketing.

Although you should be tactful *throughout* your presentation, it is most important that you avoid offending clients in your opening. Bear in mind that if you say something offensive to one person in front of others the effect is worse. So in your opening be *sensitive* not to embarrass, threaten, or insult the group. Avoid sexist, ethnic, or religious jokes.

Show respect for your clients and avoid conveying the message, "I know and you don't." Address client sensitive subjects with special care. For example, it is often preferable to say to a group, "One *concern facing insurance companies today is. . . ."* rather than "the *problem* that *you* are facing. . . ." (Please see "Relating," Page 92.)

Read the Group

Make an effort to "read" the group's reaction so you can make adjustments. One sales presenter heard a client influencer grumble about "being dragged into this with a ton of work at my desk. . . ." The presenter sensitively added into his opening, "I know the workload you are facing at this time of year, and we truly appreciate all of you taking the time this morning. . . ." This small gesture won over the grumbler, who unfolded his arms and tuned in. (Please see "Body Language," Page 87.)

Catch-up for Late Arrivers

Sometimes it is the clients who are late. Worse yet, one or two key players are not there as you begin. It is helpful to ask your client for guidance about waiting. While you do not want to penalize the clients who are there, waiting five or so minutes, especially for a senior, is to your advantage. But if you must begin without certain players present, be sure to do a quick catch-up when they walk in.

To bring key clients who arrive late up to date, *be creative and quick.* It is inappropriate to recap at great length for the late arriver, but don't ignore this person. Based on who the late arriver is, figure out which specific aspects of what you have already covered *you wish* he or she had heard and then somehow weave them into what you are covering. For example, when the head of the portfolio group walked in ten minutes late, the presenter, knowing the manager would be impressed by a top-notch client list, tactfully mentioned two prestigious clients. This got the portfolio manager's interest and attention and achieved the salesperson's objective of building credibility with this decision-maker. Always tactfully acknowledge latecomers with a slight nod, smile, and make sure they have materials. Assign a team member the responsibility of making sure late arrivers get materials. Take a moment to summarize your previous remarks, *especially* if the late arrival is the key decision-maker or influencer.

Materials

One common mistake during the opening is distributing materials even *before* you open. Avoid this unless it is logistically impossible to give out materials during the presentation. If you give out your proposals before you use them, you will find yourself competing with the material for your client's attention. Give out the proposals when you need them. *The best time to distribute materials is normally when you begin the body.* However, there are exceptions to this rule.

One engineer who won a major contract distributed his proposal as he was about to close. Initially he had been one of five competitors and now was one of two finalists. For this final presentation he slightly revised his original proposal and added as an addendum a two-inch-thick set of reprints of research articles. When he arrived to give his second presentation, he knew that only one of the five clients would not have been at his first presentation. Quickly, he devised a strategy that would "catch-up" the newcomer without taking too much time from the key points of his agenda. He briefly reviewed the first two parts of his three-part proposal, then focused on part three, the research part. Then, during part three, he discussed his credentials and *mentioned* at the *conclusion* of the presentation that he would provide the group with copies of articles as well as a copy of his original proposal. Why this approach? He felt for his second go-round neither he nor the group needed the materials, but he gave group members the opportunity to review the information in detail after the meeting. He also knew he would get points just for preparing the two inch plus packets. His strategy of withholding his materials until the end of his second presentation worked. He won the three-year contract.

There are also occasions when because of your read of the situation (major changes in the situation or players) that you decide not to distribute the proposals you prepared. If, for example, you learn early in your presentation that a key assumption you made about the client is no longer true, you might say, "Based on. . .I would like to revise the information. . . ." Of course, most often you will distribute your materials, but the point is to give them out *when you need them,* not before, and to withhold them if the situation changes.

Your Presence during the Opening

Because you are apt to be most nervous during the opening, you need to take steps to help maintain your presence. With so many look-alike products out there, the burden of differentiating your idea increasingly falls on you as the salesperson. In today's competitive environment it is increasingly difficult to separate the seller from the product. This problem compounds when selling to a group. The product and the seller become even more inseparable in a group-selling setting because all eyes are on you. And the level of personal scrutiny from clients is at its highest during the opening. Even if you are seated, you will be on "center stage." Remember, clients will be absorbing a total picture and may miss your opening words. They will be too busy judging how you look, how you carry yourself, and how genuine, prepared, and confident you are. Since this total picture gets considered and graded, *everything* (what you say, how you say it, and how you look) adds up—for or against you. It is important to appear confident and comfortable. Using eye contact and being ready with your "natural" opening should help a great deal.

Your goal should be to project confidence without conveying arrogance. By looking at and speaking to first one individual, then another at brief three-to-five second intervals, you will be able to let your comfortable one-on-one self come through. This will also let you *observe* what is going on and help you make adjustments in pace or positioning. (Please see "Body Language," Page 87.)

Think about your appearance. For example, must you wear your reading glasses as you start? The answer is no, unless you are reading a direct quote. Take off half-glasses for reading so that you do not "look down" on the group. When one presenter was asked by a colleague why he wore those half-glasses throughout his presentation, he said, "Because I had to read some figures." He read those figures about ten minutes before he closed!

Two body positions to avoid when you open are: folding your arms over your chest (as an Irish poet phrased it, "nursing your wrath"), and stuffing both hands in your pockets (an inappropriately casual gesture that will draw your client's attention and criticism). Also avoid jingling keys or change or other nervous gestures. These telltale signs will be evaluated. (Please see "Appearance" Page 85.)

When you stand, stand straight with both feet planted firmly on the floor, at least 15 inches apart; or if you sit, sit upright without letting your back rest against the back of the chair. Do not slouch or lean.

Depending on the size of the group, the formality of the situation and the format of your presentation, you can decide whether you should stand or sit among the group as you open. Standing offers the advantage of making you the focus of attention, whereas sitting creates a sense of equality. If standing, you may find a U-shaped configuration for the group most conducive to interaction with you. Stand slightly to the right or left of dead center. Do not "hide" behind things such as overhead equipment or a podium, since they will form barriers between you and the clients. When you are standing, hold your arms straight at your sides or bent at the elbows so that you are in a position to move and make gestures with your arms naturally. You can hold a pen, your glasses, or your note cards. (Please see "Body Language," Page 87.)

While you can use notes throughout the presentation, try not to refer to them during the first two or three minutes of the opening. But do not memorize your opening words—they will sound like a lifeless script. As you use notes, hold several sheets of paper, since one loose piece of paper can appear flimsy and reveal nervous trembling. Better yet, attach notes to a tablet or folder or use 3 × 5 note cards.

TO RECAP

As you open, remember:

- *Be fully prepared,* but natural. Plan how you will open but do not memorize your opening.

- Arrive early to break the ice and build rapport one-on-one.
- Don't drag out your opening! Keep it *short* and well thought-out. Be sharp and on point.
- As you begin to speak, *look at one individual* at a time. Speak to each person in intervals of three to five seconds.
- Introduce yourself, your team members (unless everyone already knows one another), and your organization. As you introduce your team members briefly explain their areas and roles in the presentation *as they relate to the client.*
- Introduce your organization unless everyone in the client group has worked with you before. Highlight your institution's benefits as they relate to the client. Keep it short.
- Be genuine as you thank the group for the opportunity to present. Allow feelings to accompany the words.
- *Do not read to clients,* unless it is a quotation.
- Find and use a "natural opening" to gain the client's interest.
- Refer to people by name when appropriate, and maintain individual eye contact. Be conscious of your gestures and appearance, especially in the beginning. The impression you make in the first few minutes will stick. Clients may miss specific words during your opening, but they will be building an overall impression of you.
- The opening is one part of the big picture. Keep it in perspective.
- Remember, your clients may forget *your exact words,* but they will not forget their overall impression of *you.*

The Group Selling Framework

Opening

- Greeting, Thank You, Introductions.
- Give a brief background.
- Use your natural opening.
- State your objective and purpose.
- Tell the clients "What's in it for them."
- Maintain your presence.

THE AGENDA AND
AGENDA CHECK

Too often salespeople take their clients on a "Magical Mystery Tour," during their presentations. If you do this, you risk being off track, you miss the chance to create a cohesive group, and you lose the opportunity to establish yourself as a leader in the group.

In the agenda phase you should give your clients a run-through of the topics to come. In the opening phase you establish rapport and interest. In the agenda phase you establish your program. *It is at this point that you can finally state the infamous lines, "Today I am (we are) going to discuss. . . .",* then bullet the key topics you plan to cover. For example, if you have five items you plan to cover, here is the place to state them so the clients get a look at the total picture and, more importantly, get a chance to make sure their agenda needs are met.

In a *final presentation* your agenda items will be more specific. For example, you may say, "Our experience in your industry, the approach we would take to . . . , your objectives, the product, our team, and how we would work with you, pricing, and a roll out schedule." But for an *initial capabilities* presentation your agenda will most likely be more general and would also include your desire to learn about the client. For example, ". . . who we are, our experience in your industry, our capabilities, our structure and team approach, but most importantly, learn the things that are key to you . . ."

Like the opening, the agenda should be brief, taking only a few minutes. Don't prolong it or the clients will get restless. Think of the agenda as a "checklist" with brief annotations. The reason the agenda is so important is that a group of clients needs more guideposts to keep it together, more than one client does. Briefly outlining your agenda you will help create a sense of group. You will help prepare the clients for what is to come, show them the thoroughness of your program.

As you present your agenda, your goal is not to persuade the clients of anything yet. It is to show them how prepared you are, give them an overview, set expectations, and then in the *agenda check* get their feedback. The agenda phase lets you check (agenda check) with the clients to determine *how your agenda meets their expectations.* This gently begins the give-and-take process. This one small gesture of briefly outlining helps because most of your competitors will fail to do this. Instead, they will proceed with the "lights out": clients won't know where they are going and they won't know how the clients are responding.

There are four tasks to be accomplished in the agenda phase of the framework:

- *Identify the Purpose of the Presentation:* Include client benefits and interests.
- *Present Your Agenda:* Identify/bullet the key points you will cover.
- *Do an Agenda Check:* Check if your agenda meets the client expectations.
- *Distribute Your Proposal:* Distribute proposal or materials (if appropriate).

REVIEW AGENDA POINTS

If you wish to have clients refer to copies of the agenda in your proposal, you can distribute your proposal. My preference, unless the agenda itself is the main document, is to verbally review the agenda and to hold on to the proposals until *after* the need check or when you are ready to use the proposal.

To give clients an overview of what you plan to cover, list several "bulleted" points. The points should be numerous enough to show substance, yet few enough to be memorable. A suggested range is four to six. These topics usually correspond to the categories (tabs) in your proposal. To lead into these points you might say, "and today we will be covering our knowledge of this market, our track record, and how we can work with you to achieve X . . . and then we'll present the financing structure. . . ."

CHECK THE AGENDA

Once you have "bulleted" the key points (not more than four, five or so) in your agenda, you should ask a question to ascertain how well the agenda matches the clients' expectations. The golden rule of one-on-one selling applies here: *Give* before you *get*.

At this stage it is time to get. You will have given when you open and describe your agenda. Now you should be ready to receive/listen, the hardest part of group selling.

Most salespeople fail to check and get feedback on what clients think of their agenda at this early point. This is bad news for salespeople who fail to do this and good news for salespeople who do, since those who seek feedback will immediately begin to distinguish themselves as listeners. *There is only one thing worse than clients who do not listen and that is clients who do not talk!* Checking client attitudes early is a small but powerful way to start the talking.

One good question to ask to check the agenda is, *"Does that meet your expectations?"* or *"Will this provide you with what you need to know?"* The objective of the agenda check is always the same: to check if your agenda matches what your client expects/needs! You don't want and won't get a long drawn out discussion here. You simply want to check and then use client information *later* in your presentation. The process of checking (asking the client a question to get feedback and input) is much more important in group selling than in one-on-one selling. In group selling situations, clients are less apt to speak up, and it is more difficult to read questions or concern in the faces of several clients. Whether a client has a minor question or a major reservation or objection, he or she often keeps it quiet in a group setting. It is your job to get it out of the clients by checking. If a client is opposed to you he or she may jump in to attack, and if one client is all for you he or she may jump in or help rescue you—but don't count on either. You must ask for reactions. Whether your audience is hostile, friendly, or indifferent, your clients think they are there to listen. It is your job to get them to talk.

If you have done your homework, it is unlikely that someone will be dissatisfied with your *general* agenda. Problems can occur, however, if by chance you have missed a major point, if your client liaison has not prepared the client group, if the clients do not understand what is meant by a particular heading, or if there has been a real misunderstanding. During your agenda check you have the opportunity to make adjustments or to promise further explanation. For example, if a client asks, "Will you be covering the tax implications?" you can say, "Yes. This is an important point. In. . . , I plan to cover it." but *you must not go into detail* at this time. If you had not planned to go on to the point, you may acknowledge this and promise follow-through either during the presentation or later: "I hadn't planned to detail that but I would be happy to . . . Thank you for bringing it up."

In another situation, the head of a hospital asked if build-out costs would be covered. The lead presenter was not prepared to discuss it. Fortunately, however, he was quick thinking enough to look in the direction of one of his team members who had been assigned from their architectural division who would be able to discuss it in depth. This colleague said, as if on cue, "Yes. That's something I will cover when we get to . . . "

Agenda check does *not* come naturally to most salespeople. Asking questions to a group seems to be more difficult for most people than asking questions one-on-one. But checking is indispensable, so steel yourself and *do it*.

Many salespeople resist checking because they are afraid that if they check, the client will throw a monkey wrench into their agenda. Even so, checking is worthwhile. Imagine the worst situation, when a client totally rejects the agenda saying something like, "We certainly are *not* considering. . . ." or states an objection or asks a hostile question. It is better to know sooner than later. You will at least have the opportunity to get additional information, and make the adjustment, or (in the worse scenario) adjourn.

Other salespeople resist checking because they think it will cost them too much time. These salespeople should weigh the benefit of having almost 100% of the air time as they make their A to Z presentation, against the risk of losing the client permanently somewhere along the alphabet path. As one senior investment banker says, "I tell my people, 'Right after you present your agenda, find out if it meets the clients' expectations, find out what they think, and keep a dialogue going. *The less the client talks, the less likely you'll close.*' "

A consultant tells how he literally saved a sale by an agenda check. When he asked if the agenda was O.K., the client decision-maker, one of seven clients sitting around the table, said, "I'm tired of hearing about your long-standing relationship with us. We are not interested in. . . . Your firm hasn't had an original idea in eight years." This was the first time this salesperson had met this particular senior client. He had no idea that such hostility existed. The room became tense. The salesperson took a breath and said softly, "Certainly I am interested in your views on this and I appreciate your candor. I think we have several options at this time: I could pack up and leave, which I truly hope is not the case; I could present the proposal I came with; or we could have a frank discussion about how all of you feel about this." He then remained *silent*. They had the frank discussion and he walked out with a very large, three-year, six-figure contract. Checking his agenda allowed him to deal with the objection and reposition what he had to say.

The only possible downside of asking for input or direction is that some groups just will not talk. Since the agenda-check question can be somewhat of a formality, you may not get more than a few nodding heads indicating agreement. While this can be disconcerting, you can handle it. If clients do not respond, *do not press hard for feedback*. Wait several seconds and if there is no comment, deal with silence from clients gracefully by saying, "Fine, please feel free to raise any points as we go along." Of course, when no input is forthcoming, a little red flag should go up in your head. Lack of response may signal problems, or it may simply indicate that the group is quiet, shy, noncommittal, tough, or neutral. It is your job to tread lightly and figure out what is going on.

Not only will checking allow you to adjust your sales presentation to client needs, it sets the pattern of give-and-take, it tells the clients they have a choice, and it subtly shows respect for the client. What you are really asking is, "Is this agenda O.K. with you?" By giving clients a choice, you *increase* their receptivity and reduce their resistance. It's like a mirror—how you respond to clients is how they will respond to you. When clients do participate in the checking phase, you will have ideas that you can weave into your point when you get them. You can give the client credit by relating your point to their comment. You can say, "Frank, as you mentioned earlier, indemnification. . . . We see. . . ."

TO RECAP

- Distribute your proposal (if you plan to use it at this time).
- State your purpose.
- List the key points you will cover.
- Check if the agenda meets the expectation of the group.
- Thank clients for input when they give it.
- Comment on how/when you will address their points, but do *not* go into detail until later.

The Group Selling Framework

Agenda/Agenda Check

- "Today I'm going to discuss. . . ."
- Highlight 3 or 4 topic areas.
- "How does that meet your expectations?"
- Remember: Keep it brief! Do not go into detail. This is not your presentation.

CLIENT NEED CHECK

The need check is designed to go deeper than the agenda check. Even after you have presented your agenda and checked it against your client's expectations, you are not ready to move into the body of your presentation. Once you have checked, *ask the clients to highlight what is most important to them.* Remember, your presentation is not the alphabet song. Each letter should not get equal weight and the pieces may not come in order. To help you know where to put emphasis with the group, let the clients identify what they care about most so you can place emphasis on what matters to them. Sometimes the agenda check will lead into this naturally; but if it doesn't, you need to ask the group this penetrating question—"To help get the balance of our presentation right, may I ask what areas you would like us to focus on or what specific concerns you have?" Asking a question like this to get input from the clients takes discipline and courage, especially if you don't know everyone in the room. But this is precisely when your checking for client needs is most crucial. Your goal *throughout* your presentation is to create give-and-take, which will allow for more spontaneity and comfort. It will enable you to differentiate your product/idea by relating it to the *client's situation.* Again, if the clients are not forthcoming with information, don't get rattled; just say, "Well, please feel free to ask questions or bring up points as we go."

The information and client contact you had prior to your presentation will determine how indepth your need question should be. The need check question is even more important in a capabilities presentation. In these situations you must extend the need check question by adding questions aimed at *identify-*

ing needs such as, "What is important to you in a research firm . . . ? What type of studies are you currently doing? What kind of methodologies . . . ?" But even in situations in which you have previously identified needs with the client, you should give the *group* the opportunity to underscore its concerns. By identifying needs *before* you launch into your presentation you will be able to position what you say.

No Monologues!

Presenters who skip this critical stage begin their descent into what can be a fatal trap, one that can also occur in one-on-one selling—making a monologue *product sale* rather than a dialogue or "multilogue" *need sale.* In a monologue sale a presenter goes from A to Z. A presentation shaped by a need check is more tailored to the client and more relevant. And the need check can help stimulate the group involvement so critical to differentiating your presentation and winning more deals.

In today's environment, straight product selling is no longer viable. As has been stated before, the features and benefits of competitive products often sound alike to clients. Frequently clients say they cannot differentiate one competitive product from another. Even salespeople have a hard time differentiating their own products. Even if you have the luxury of having a unique idea or product, it is not likely to remain unique for very long in today's competitive environment. A little more than a decade ago the product was the differentiator, but this is not so today. Differentiation occurs as much or more *outside* the product in things such as service, expertise, strategy, flexibility, track record, and most importantly in the salesperson/sales team, rather than *inside* the product in its "hard" features and benefits. Product differentiation is also possible by how the saleperson relates the product to the client needs. But to leverage this, salespeople need to understand the client's situation so they can *tailor* their presentations accordingly. If you fall back on making a monologue, A to Z presentation with little or no feedback from the clients until the Q&A you will risk making generic presentations that sound like everyone else's presentation.

By getting the group to talk early before you plunge into your idea, you can begin the *crafting* process of matching your idea to the client's needs and perceptions. Both the agenda check and the need check show that you respect the client and recognize that the client's needs supercede your own. By asking clients what they want emphasized you can avoid the impossible and presumptuous task of divining the client's thoughts.

The need check as a way to begin give-and-take has other benefits. It reduces the pressure on you to perform. It also allows for more spontaneity. And like the Q&A it allows for a match-up of what the salesperson says and what the clients need to know. Some useful ways to start include: "Now that I have gone over the agenda, to help us focus on the most important items of our agenda. . .", "To use our time on areas most important to you. . . .", "Since I have not met with all of you. . . .", "Since I want to address the points most important to you . . .", "Since we haven't met as a group before. . . .", or "We have a full agenda. To make sure I spend time on the aspects most important to you, which points . . . what concerns. . . ." These leads can create the give-and-take ambience of the Q&A throughout your presentation. Your objective in the need check is to get the clients to tell you what they want covered, where they want emphasis, how they are thinking, and what they need. Keep in mind you are unlikely to sell anything to anyone if you do not know how they think.

Some salespeople argue against this approach, defending their reluctance to ask a need check question with classic excuses: "Look, I've done my homework and, therefore, this is unnecessary." "They'll think I'm not prepared.", "There is no time.", "I'll lose control.", "They'll think we are too manipulative." One seasoned sales presenter went so far as to say that his A to Z monologue style of presenting was his method of "crowd control." Another who feared appearing reported that the feedback his team got as to why they did not win a deal in a "bake-off" (final competition) was that they were "too arrogant." Had he asked for feedback on his agenda he may have appeared "human." *It takes guts to check.* There really is no danger of losing control or ground if you know how to ask for and deal with input from clients. Here's how.

One way to help both you and the client feel comfortable with checking is to preface the question with the reason *why* you are asking the question. You can reassure the client that this need check is not a substitute for homework by prefacing your need-check question with comments like, *"So I get the balance of my presentation right,* what . . . ?" Prefacing statements will mollify the clients and make them more willing to participate. Prefacing will help make it clear you are seeking emphasis not attempting to uncover fundamental needs.

Keep in mind that you may not have met some individuals. This will give you a chance to understand their perspective. And especially when you are making an *introduction capabilities presentation* to a prospective client as opposed to a final competitive presentation, the needs check is even *more* important.

Although you need to keep things moving, don't rush too quickly through the need check. While there is no prescribed amount of time that should be dedicated to the need check in an hour presentation, a minimum of five minutes is a healthy sign. This time should be spent noting needs, *not* addressing them. Listen and acknowledge the points in an appreciative way. Make a brief comment recognizing the importance of the point, then state when you will cover it. You may wish to jot down all the points and who made them. This will help you incorporate them into your comments later, and to relate with your eyes, your words, or both the points to the clients who raised them.

The feedback from the need check will help you position your ideas throughout your presentation. For example you could say, "Yes, tax liability is a major consideration and I will cover that. . . ." "We have tables which I will review. . . ." or "Yes, Tom, we have given thought to the offshore implications and we actually ran the numbers. I will cover XYZ in depth when. . . ." "Thank you." or "Mac, when you mentioned. . .in Florida. . .and here we can. . . ." Once you get input from the clients, you need to remember to incorporate the information appropriately and to decide how to weigh your presentation. Tom Peter's book *In Search of Excellence* made the phrase "stay close to the customer" a corporate catch phrase. Checking needs at the beginning and throughout your presentation is a way to verbally do just that.

Once you get input from *one* client, don't fall into the trap of assuming that that is all there is. After the first client speaks, ask again, "What *other* points do you want me to focus on?" or "What other concerns are there?" But, again, *do not belabor the point; keep the pace moving.* Do not call on anyone. This is volunteers only! Do not put anyone on the spot or create a "stand off."

As an aside, the client who speaks first after (or before) you ask your need check question is often the key decision-maker or a powerful influencer, whether or not this corresponds with the organization chart. Two cues to help you determine this are: how attentive others are when this person speaks, and how the client positions his or her remarks. For example, key decision-makers often begin or end their comments by encouraging other team members to feel free to speak up, correct them, or comment on what they have said. However, the more "powerful" the speaker, the less likely colleagues are to do so.

Hopefully, most of the time you will get client input, but if your group is silent during the agenda check and remains uncommunicative in the need check, again, handle the silence gracefully by encouraging clients to ask questions as they arise. For example, "Well, please feel free to ask questions you may have *throughout* our meeting."

Invite Client Questions

One final task remains before you move onto the body of your sales presentation. You should give the client group guidelines about *how and when* to ask questions. In a group selling situation, client questions and interaction are essential, so while you should tell the clients that there will be a short Q&A period at the end of the presentation, *you should invite the group to ask questions throughout your sales presentation*—and mean it! Every group sell should have a Q&A period as a safety net. But if you wait to deal with all client questions until the end in a Q&A, you may find you have insufficient time to unravel misconceptions, misunderstandings, questions, concerns, and objections built up over the hour or so in which you have presented. But remember this invitation does not remove the need for you to check (such as, "Any questions before I move on?") throughout your presentation. (Please see "Q&A," Page 54.)

Only under very unusual circumstances, such as highly political situations or when your presentation is a formality, might you want to curtail client questions and client involvement.

TO RECAP

• After checking the agenda, ask clients to highlight needs and concerns so that you can focus on what is most important to them.

• Acknowledge and show appreciation for their input, *but do not discuss details on each issue on the spot.*

• Explain there will be a Q&A at the conclusion. (Please see Page 54 for "Q&A".)

• Invite clients to ask questions *throughout* your presentation.

The Group Selling Framework

Client Need Check

• "Of the agenda items we've covered, what is of particular interest . . . where do you want us to focus?"
• "What are you currently . . . ?"
• "What other areas . . . focus. . .?"
• Create a give-and-take atmosphere.
• "We will hold time for a Q&A at the conclusion, but please feel free to ask questions or raise points throughout the presentation."
• Remember: Getting clients to help you set your focus will give you an edge. It will creat client participation and enable you to position.

THE BODY OF THE SALES PRESENTATION

"Then let's begin with. . ." are the words you can use to move into the body of your sales presentation. The body of your sales presentation is its heart, the place to present your ideas as a match to your client's needs. It will consume the bulk of your time, often as much as 35 to 40 minutes of an hour presentation. While you need to open, present your agenda, and check for needs, *you need to get to the body* of your presentation fairly quickly. This is where your preparation, your depth of knowledge about the client as well as your own capabilities, and your skill at delivery will shine through. The body is where you tell your story—where the essence of what you can do and how you can do it gets communicated. Highly flexible, the body is made up of features and benefits, both the tangible and intangible ones.

The key to the body, the "crux" of your sales presentation, is to *keep your client involved*. Not only will this help you craft your ideas as you go through your proposal and keep you on track with the clients, it will also create client buy-in. While you and your ideas will be under scrutiny, creating give-and-take during the body will help take the focus off you and place it on the discussion. With a "multilogue" going on you personally as the presenter will be subject to less personal scrutiny from the clients because when clients are involved they "sit in judgement" less.

Your goal, however, since you are selling to a group and not selling one-on-one, is *not* to create the 50%/50%, one-on-one selling mix where you share the talk/listen time equally with the client. First, the larger number of clients in the group make it more difficult to orchestrate a discussion. Second, you need to tell your story since your clients have gathered as a group to hear what you have to recommend or say and they rightly expect to hear recommendations for a final presentation or your capabilities for an introductory presentation. The combination of trying to orchestrate a multi-client discussion and telling your story to help clients make a decision usually makes an even-steven exchange inappropriate. You should, however, aim for *at least* a 70 percent (you) to 30 percent (client) mix. Unfortunately, many salespeople in group selling situations resort to a 95 percent-to-5 percent mix (95 percent salespersons speaking and 5 percent clients speaking) and talk themselves right out of the sale.

One of the greatest errors salespeople make when they are selling to a group is that they take the word "presentation" literally to mean "something presented; a descriptive or persuasive account (as by a salesman of his product). . . ." (*Webster's*). *Webster's* equates selling with talking. This definition looks at selling as product selling and creates a presentation as one-way communication.

Your task today, however, is to make sure this doesn't happen. You need to change the role of the client from one of absorbing information to sharing information. You need to go from "telling" to "interviewing." By making yourself more porous through checking and questioning, you will help the clients open up. In today's buyer's market, straight *product* selling (lecturing/educating) cannot compete with mutual sharing in which all parties listen to one another. Tactfully you can create participation and get feedback. *While you are still responsible for the presentation, part of your job is to foster client participation.*

As you involve the client, you create the "give-and-take" ease. By asking questions and checking, you will be able to get feedback that will allow you to position your ideas and build clilent commitment. One exception to getting input would be when the salesperson is so greatly respected and distinguished for his or her expertise that clients sit back and listen. In today's instant catch-up environment and with the ever-increasing level of client sophistication, this kind of expertise and acceptance is rare. Another exception would be when you read the group and sense strong hostility. If you are getting stonewalled, don't continue to ask for feedback; but if you cannot turn this around regardless of how hard you try, you will have little hope of selling.

STRUCTURING INFORMATION IN THE BODY

How you structure the body of your presentation should be determined by your objectives, the culture of the client, and the amount of time you have. It is better to cover key parts in appropriate depth than to try to say it all and run on or run over. (Please see "Timing," Page 148.)

While this will be covered in greater depth in the chapter, "Developing the Presentation Package" (Page 161), let's look at a sequence for structuring your presentation. In general, you should begin the body with a brief recap of the *client's objective and needs* as you understand them. Starting with the client can be one way to differentiate your presentation. For example, when a well-known developer was asked why he opted to do the deal with one firm over another, he said, "They were the *only* ones who began the discussion of their idea by talking about *our objectives and about our market place.* They convinced us they really understood the Boston real estate market and what could be done here." Once you present the client's objectives, you can state your purpose. In the body you should detail your idea, continuously matching it to the client's objectives while referring to the "hot" needs and issues you have uncovered through your preparation and in your need check.

Your pricing discussion is an important part of the body, but this should be presented only *after* you have presented your idea and linked it to the clients' needs. If you bring out the price tag before you bring out the merchandise, you will sabotage your sale by discussing price without discussing value. As you present your pricing, present your *value in helping the clients meet their objectives and discuss the factors that differentiate you.* In stating your price, be confident: inch up in your chair or stand straight, and keep an even, strong voice. In today's competitive environment, clients buy neither products nor price alone. They buy what they believe will enable them to reach their objectives. Therefore, don't separate price from value. Also, if a client begins to negotiate with you in the presence of the entire client group, depending of course on the specific situation, it is often advisable to table the negotiation by saying "Let me give this consideration." (or) "Let me make note of this so I can get back to you quickly." Negotiating in public can kill client flexibility; the ego becomes as much the issue as the figures or terms when clients take a position from which they cannot easily retreat.

One savvy team of three presenters structured its presentation to maximize the strengths of each of its members and to position their idea most effectively. Their structure looked like this:

Sales Team	Part of Group Selling Framework	
Salesperson #1	OPENING • Introduction AGENDA NEED CHECK	
Salesperson #2	BODY • Knowledge of Boston Market • Idea	Client Discussion Maintained throughout the Presentation
Salesperson #3	BODY • Pricing SUMMARY	
Salespeople #1, #2, #3 Salesperson #3	Q&A CLOSE	

Each time you cover a key point before advancing to the next point, remember to check for questions or comments. Your goal is to keep the presentation interactive. The six critical skills covered later in this book will serve as the communication tools you will use throughout the presentation. While all of the six critical skills are just that, critical, one skill will help you maintain give and take during the presentation: checking. Checking throughout the presentation (asking for feedback, questions, reactions) is one of the best ways to get client feedback and create the give-and-take you need. Checking is courteous—"May I ask if there are any questions before we move on?" Checking is brave—"How does that sound?" It is smart— "Which of the two approaches interests you. . . ?" It is respectful—"Is there anything that should be covered in more detail or anything I wasn't clear on?" Each time you cover a major point in the body ask, "What questions do you have, before I move on?" *This checking before moving on is critical.* One presenter, to his regret, explained a complicated deal structure, then proceeded to move on to pricing without asking if there were any questions. The objections and difficulties he encountered during the pricing discussion clearly revealed that the client group hadn't the slightest idea how the structure worked. Had these questions been resolved prior to discussing price, the group's aggressive price resistance could have tempered or even eliminated.

DIFFERENTIATE YOUR IDEA

As you work through the body of your presentation, you will have a special challenge: differentiating your product/idea. The look-alike product environment you are selling in has pushed differentiation outside the product to things such as service, quality, and fit with the client. Differentiation is a major problem today for most salespeople, as a topnotch firm recently learned "on the job." After winning a deal, the managing director was given copies of his two competing proposals. After studying the proposals, he concluded that the ideas, pricing, and even the proposal formats were almost identical. He mused, "Maybe they (the client) just flipped a coin." Of course, clients don't flip coins. But they don't strictly buy products. When the features and benefits of proposals look alike, it is the salesperson/sales team who is the differentiator. Recognizing this, the managing director arranged for himself and his salespeople to participate in sales-presentation training and engaged a marketing/promotion specialist to help spruce up their proposal format to give his team every possible edge.

By extreme contrast, one participant in a sales presentation seminar insisted that his product was a commodity, impossible to differentiate. Yet he was at a loss to explain why his competitors won his business with their almost-identical products and almost-identical pricing. He failed to understand that while his basic product *may* have been a commodity, *the client was not a commodity and neither was he or his firm.* By positioning his product relative to what the client wanted to achieve and communicating how *his* own firm could be the ONE to help the client achieve it, he may have been able to close. His results indicated that at least one of his competitors was doing something he was not. He finally accepted the fact that the client does ultimately perceive differences, but those differences often are *outside* the product—in the client and in the sales organization and salesperson or sales team.

Your institution, your team, your knowledge, your experience, your knowledge of your client—are ways to differentiate yourself. AT&T, technology personified, in its 1988 "signature" TV ad campaign shows a series of its customer service representatives waxing enthusiastically about what they *personally* do for their customers. And for its corporate clients AT&T sells "a system" that defies obsolescence and calms client fears about inflexibility. More and more products today contain intangibles that not only require, but *are* after-sales satisfaction and service. Even tangible products like computers have intangible service and capability aspects strong enough to swing the sale.

One leading investment bank accents its performance capabilities by using an advertisement that one of its prestigious Fortune 500 clients placed in the *New York Times* which proudly publicized its relationship with this investment bank. Although the ad is now several years old, the investment banker who worked with this account distributes copies of it during his presentations to set himself apart and add to his credibility. Products can almost always be differentiated if you look deeply enough at your product, your client, and your organization and yourself. Product differentiation exists *inside* and *outside* the product and *within* the client.

"Outside" product differentiation involves things like your track record, your level of quality, services, your execution capabilities and expertise. Even when your client list "speaks for itself," remember it needs your voice. If your structure is your strength—for example if you don't separate sales from execution giving the client far better more timely service. Remind the clients they will see you and your team throughout the deal, and that it won't be turned over to juniors. Whatever your product advantage is, *you* must show it to set yourself apart. One smaller telecommunication firm won a major contract using both inside and outside features and benefits. Knowing the client wanted not only *one* company who could play the integrator role, but also needed quality service and responsiveness, the salesperson built his presentation around reliability (the most reliable in the industry) and support (a call *each* month to check the client's satisfaction). He also presented a system that could expand the present solution to other needs, for example providing one telephone number across townships.

The body is the place to present this kind of information. Certainly, if you have unique product advantages emphasize them. And whether or not they are unique, be sure to cover the features and benefits that are important to the client so that the client has a clear idea of what you can do and how you do it. Selectively focus on the features and benefits relevant to the client. Your group selling presentation should contain client benefits, not just features. But a laundry list of features and benefits are of interest to few clients. Focus on those of importance to the clients. By weaving in the benefits relating to what clients want to achieve and want to know, you will be able to make them enthusiastic about what you can do. Also, since clients have varying degrees of knowledge, positioning benefits will help less sophisticated clients understand what the technical features mean. For example, one person in the group may not understand the implications of the spread you depict in a chart, but he or she is likely to understand what saving 50 basis points—or better yet, an exact dollar figure such as $420,000— means to the bottom line.

Relevant benefit selling, related to needs, is like the language of love—everyone understands it. Rather than commenting in-depth on a complex chart, *although you do get points for having developed the chart,* it is far better in most situations to refer to the chart and then focus on the benefits to the client and the questions the clients may have about the chart. You should spend much less time going through the details of a chart than you might think. Checking with clients, "What questions do you have on how we derived the savings of fifty basis points?" will save you from wasting time and boring clients.

Be clear, accurate, and concise as you present relevant features and benefits. Use examples or analogies to help make your point. For example, one insurance agent got "stuck" each time he tried to explain to clients why it was dangerous to switch their director and officer (D + O) liability insurance. When he brought this problem up with his manager, the manager suggested he explain the risk to the client by comparing it to a "pre-condition" clause in health insurance, because that was a situation that everyone could easily relate to. It worked! Along with examples, use visuals during the body if you need them to illustrate complex points or trigger discussion points. (Please see "Visuals," Page 178.)

Establishing Credibility

The final big-ticket decision usually boils down to *trust:* Who can do it? Who can do it best? As all consumers know, although they sometimes learn it the hard way, even look-alike products are different. Unfortunately, as the advertisement for *Consumer Report* reminds the consumer, "It's not until you get the product home that you learn how good it is." That is one reason why track record and referrals are so powerful in selling. They are the closest thing the client can get to "getting the product home." References and examples can build credibility and give life to the body of your presentation. But don't go into a story willy-nilly, and don't exaggerate. Practice so that you don't ramble. Keep examples short and to the point. In addition to personal examples, use research results from your own firm as well as from outside sources, experts' opinions such as your economist, client quotations ("One of our clients in Ohio said. . . .)", analogies, illustrations, sample transactions, statistical data, references or whatever else can support your idea or bolster your credibility.

Experience is a great persuader. A simple comment like *"In our experience. . ."* can boost client confidence tremendously. One investment banker who was asked three times by the chairman, "Will you do it at 94?" replied *each* time, "Based on our experience in. . .the market, our recommendation is to do it at 93. We think that the deal will unravel at 94." This Fortune 500 company did the deal at 93! His preparation and confidence convinced the client. As much as the clients are judging what you have to say, they are evaluating you and asking themselves, "Do I want this person (organization) to be the one next to me for this deal?"

Homework is essential to credibility, and it shows through in the body. For example, a salesperson representing a training company won a half-million-dollar telemarketing training contract not because the client viewed the nuts and bolts of his training programs as different, but because he was the only one of five competitors who demonstrated that his firm would get to know the client and customize the training. The salesperson had called the client's 800 number six times before his presentation to find out firsthand how the salesforce was performing. While he did not offend the client with the gory details of the worst mistakes the salespeople made when answering the calls, he covered general strengths and weaknesses and demonstrated how he would address the specific needs of the salesforce. He said, "Over the past several days, we called your 800 number to get a feel for how your people are selling now. What we found were knowledgeable and friendly salespeople—very eager to help. As you know and as we discussed earlier, salespeople tend to bypass questions and qualifying. They were so anxious to tell their story. . . ." He positioned the client's strengths and areas for improvement in a way that made the client comfortable and eager to work with them.

Above all, credibility means that when you don't have an answer, you don't fabricate it. While of course, you should be as prepared as possible, especially for a final presentation and you *must* be able to think fast on your feet, you should not fabricate information. If you come up short, acknowledge you don't have the specific information, find out details of what the client needs to know, and set a specific time to get back to him or her and the others.

HANDLING LATECOMERS

As you make your presentation, notice who comes in and who leaves. Sometimes when you are in the midst of the body of your presentation you may have to back up to do a *brief* summary and a needs check if a key player walks in late. A banker and his two colleagues were presenting to six clients. About 20 minutes into their sales presentation, a man entered the room. Immediately, the banker stood up, reached across the table to shake hands, stated his name, introduced his teammates and in three minutes summarized what had transpired to that point. He then asked if the person had any specific areas he wanted addressed. The latecomer was the chairman, the economic decision-maker. Fortunately, the banker was not only familiar with the chairman's picture from the annual report, but was able to read the room. He saw how the clients looked up and respectfully acknowledged the latecomer and made room for him around the table. Without his homework and group reading ability, the salesperson may have lost this opportunity to make points with the chairman.

USING PROPOSAL AND HANDOUTS

Since you will probably need to use your proposal and handouts throughout the body of your presentation, you should know how to use them to your advantage. Distribute your proposal as you begin the body, if you have not already done so. Although this will be covered in depth later the key points are:

- *structure your written proposal* to follow the general order of your oral presentation so that you can avoid unnecessary jumping back and forth

- *use your proposal flexibly*—don't become a page by page slave to it
- *do not read* to your clients during the body of your presentation, unless you are reading a specific direct quotation, figures, new, or technical information
- *use notes or note cards* in a bulleted format; jot notes in the margin of your proposal copy, or use overheads as your outline.

Handouts can become roadblocks if used incorrectly. Take the case of the salesperson who at the end of what seemed to be a good presentation to four clients, opened his briefcase and said, "We have a new brochure, let me give one to you," handing a brochure to the treasurer and ignoring the assistant treasurer and two junior finance people who were also around the table. When explaining why a competing company got the business, the client did not talk about product superiority but said, "They didn't impress me. The second guy on the team didn't say *one* word. But what really turned me off was at the end the salesman opened his briefcase and handed *me* a brochure. He ignored Alice, Barbara, and John. I could see he had 20 of those brochures in his briefcase. The fact that he ignored my people told me something about how he would work with them. Even if he had only one, he should have apologized and told them he would get the brochures to them later."

TO RECAP

- Organize the key elements of your presentation with an eye toward what the client wants to achieve.
- Use a logical but sales-oriented sequence, for example, features and benefits/value before price.
- Use but do not read your proposal (except for figures and technical information).
- Create a dialogue (approximate 70/30 mix).
- Make sure the amount of information fits into your allotted time. (Please see "Time," Page 150.)
- Position/personalize the information to your client's needs and use benefits.
- Organize key elements in a client-oriented, logical sequence.

The Group Selling Framework

Body

- "Then let's begin with. . . ."
- The body is the ♡ of your presentation.
- Use relevant features with benefits as they relate to the client.
- Differentiate your idea, institution, self, and client!
- Clarify and demonstrate with effective visual aids.
- Keep clients involved.
- Keep checking.
- Remember: DO NOT READ YOUR PROPOSAL!

THE SUMMARY

"In summary . . ." Believe it or not, these are compelling words for clients, but salespeople rarely capitalize on them. Many salespeople do not summarize at all; they just "wind up". The summary, however, is an element you can use to help drive your message home. Every presentation, no matter how long or short, should have a summary. Indeed, the shorter the presentation, the greater the need for an effective summary. To be on the safe side, prepare incremental summaries for each major part of the body encapsulating your key message in the event your time is cut short.

This replay of highlights offers a unique opportunity to reinforce the key *information you want the clients to walk out remembering*. If you do not take the time to think about what you want to say in advance, allowing for fine-tuning based on the discussion with the clients, you will leave it up to the clients to extract what they choose to remember.

The fine tuning is an important step in making sure the summary points are personalized to the group. Rattling off three or four generic points without tying them to the discussion that has taken place is almost as ineffective as no summary at all. For example, one articulate salesperson summarized, "We are cost-competitive. We provide quality research. And our interpretations are actionable." This summary was flat and undistinguishable. It could have come to life had he changed the sequence starting with quality which was paramount to the clients and then added detail about his role in every stage of the project.

To help develop an effective summary, ask yourself, *"What do I want my clients to walk out remembering?"* Rehearse your summary and evaluate if it has the effect you want. *Crisply* and *briefly* recap the *three or four major points* you want the client to know. The last thing you want to do is bore the group by rehashing details, so keep your summary *short*. Don't introduce any new information in the summary unless you think of a key point you forgot to mention. In this case, simply say, "Before I summarize, I'd like to present one more. . . ." As always keep the pace going but do not rush. Use pauses for emphasis. As you phrase the major points, be sure to include *CLIENT NEEDS AND BENEFITS*. Focus on what the client wants to achieve and how you will help the client achieve it.

One investment banker consistently uses his personal stamp as a part of his summaries, saying "And finally I want to stress that *Pat* and *I* will *personally* work on this project. We will see to every detail including. . . . We don't turn this over to junior people." "If you want to know who will do the things we discussed, you are looking at them."

An advertising executive went a step further in his presentation. He walked over to the door and said, "In summary, I would like you to remember three things. . . ." He then proceeded to close (almost but not quite slam) the door. Mounted on the back of the door was a placard listing three things his firm could do to "close the door" on his subject—the daily outflow of funds that the client was experiencing. While you certainly don't have to play Martin Luther by nailing your message to a door, you should use the summary to nail down your points. You can also use a visual to help register your message.

TO RECAP:

- Ask yourself, "What do I want the group to walk out remembering?"
- Say "In summary. . . ."
- Present several key points you want the client to remember linking relevant features and benefits that match what the client wants to achieve.

- Do not go into detail and do not cover any new information in your summary.
- Personalize and tailor the points in your summary.

The Group Selling Framework

Summary

- "In summary, there are three points I want to leave with you. . . ."
- Re-emphasize three or four major points.
- Personalize how you position the key summary points.
- Highlight relevant features with benefits and match with needs.
- Consider using a visual.
- Add no new information.
- Remember: EVERY PRESENTATION SHOULD HAVE A SUMMARY!

THE QUESTION AND ANSWER

No matter how interesting your sales presentation or how much *you think* you need to cover, you should be conscious of your time so that you *leave ample time* for a Q&A. The Q&A is important for several reasons: the spontaneous nature of the Q&A allows you to build credibility; salespeople who otherwise lack luster in monologue presentations can shine in the Q&A because their one-on-one self comes out; and the Q&A enables the salesperson to address what clients need to know, not what the salesperson still wants to say. But it should be mentioned some salespeople literally fall apart in the Q&A. This usually stems from 1) their *not being fully grounded in their subject,* 2) they have preconceived ideas and are set on making an A to Z presentation so that a question from a client feels like a curve ball, 3) they don't know how to answer questions in a group setting.

To maximize the spontaneity of the Q&A, reserve approximately 10 percent of your allotted time for Q&A. Of course the amount of time should be adjusted based on the meeting and your reading of the client. But remember, questions from clients throughout the presentation *do not substitute for the Q&A.* You need the *safety net* of a Q&A to catch any lingering questions or concerns and to correct possible misunderstandings.

You can begin your Q&A with, "Before I close, what remaining questions or concerns do you have. . . ." After you get an answer your first question, remember to ask again and again as long as you keep getting questions for additional questions. Your objective is to resolve any questions or concerns *while you are there to answer them.*

CAUGHT SHORT

If in the Q&A (or elsewhere in your presentation), a client asks a question you can't answer, tell the client you would like to look into the point, and ask for further clarification of what the client wants to know. If appropriate, say that you will get back to him or her and set a specific time to do so. Unfortunately, if the presentation is conclusive and clients will be making a decision immediately, you may not get this second shot. Therefore, be as prepared as possible to answer questions while you are there. Use your team members during the Q&A to maximize their expertise and involve them. *As mentioned, do not fudge your answer—because your credibility is at stake.*

NO QUESTIONS COME YOUR WAY

When clients don't ask questions during the Q&A, move to your close. If you consistently don't get questions you may not be asking for them in a convincing way. How you ask for questions can influence whether or not you get them. A nationally recognized speaker had difficulty getting questions from his audiences. By observing a tape of one of his speeches, he and his coach were able to diagnose and correct his problem: his timing and gestures told the audience that the Q&A was not important, so clients were reluctant to extend the time.

First of all, he spoke "up to the wire" and asked for questions at the precise moment his speech was scheduled to end. Second, his body language conveyed to the audience he really didn't want questions. When he asked for questions, his voice got softer, he tilted his head and he looked above the group, nonverbally saying to the group, "Take it easy on me." Thanks to coaching, he now regularly reserves at least five minutes for the Q&A. With a confident voice he says, "We have set time aside for Q&A. What questions do you have?" and the hands shoot up as expected.

While speeches are not the same as sales presentations, when it comes to Q&A, they share similar challenges and solutions, as this case shows.

How to Answer Questions

Most importantly, prepare the "content" part of your answers in advance. Develop a list of anticipated questions and get ready for the tough ones. Rehearse how you will answer them. In the words of one reputedly anti-business political candidate about to meet with the leaders of the business community, "I know the questions and I'm ready for them." But being prepared does not mean that you can go on automatic pilot when the questions come your way. It is important to *position* your information to match the client. For example, when a salesperson whose company had recently been acquired was asked how the merger was going, since the client he was addressing had also gone through a merger, he presented his story with an insider's view: "Well, as all of you know here the first year was the 'honeymoon.' Then came the market crash and things got tough. X took a more active role. We got to know each other and this was good. We have an excellent relationship now. We respect each other. . . . We make referrals to each other and send each other business."

At all times, listen to the question fully. Don't interrupt the client, and don't become defensive. *Most importantly, don't over-answer.* Keep it short. If you over-answer you will risk losing the interest of the group. Answer a question without answering related questions, going into an inappropriate level of detail, or going on a tangent. Keep your answer to the point and then check, "Does that answer your question?" Look not only at the client who asked the question, but include all other clients by also looking at them as you answer. (Please see "Questioning—Q&A, Page 98/54.)

TO RECAP

Some tips to help you maximize the Q&A are:

- Save time for the Q&A.
- Listen to the complete question.
- Thank the client for the question.
- Ask for clarification if you do not understand the question.

- Position your response. (Please see "Position," Page 111 .)
- Do not over answer. Answer the specific question completely but concisely.
- After you answer the question, check with the client asking the question, "Does this answer your question?"
- Include the group in your answer by looking at all group members as you answer.
- Do not belabor the Q&A period. If no questions are forthcoming say, "Well, I will be here . . . for any questions. . . ." (Please see Q&A Skills, Page 54.)

The Group Selling Framework

Questions & Answers

- "Before concluding, what questions or concerns do you have?"
- Answer with brevity. Do not over-answer.
- Position your response.
- Get the essence of the answer in several sentences.
- Elaborate only if necessary.
- *Check* to make sure you have really answered the question.
- Use eye contact to include everyone.
- Remember: USE YOUR ENTIRE TEAM FOR QUESTIONS AND ANSWERS.

THE CLOSE

Your summary leads you to your close; the summary is *not* the close. You lead into your close with a final check by asking if there are any remaining concerns or questions. The purpose of your close is to *express your desire to work with the clients, confirm the next appropriate step, motivate action with you, and thank the clients for their consideration.*

A seminar participant indentified her objective for the course as "closing—how to ask for the business when I am making a capabilities presentation." When asked to demonstrate how she planned to close her next presentation, she confidently and articulately said, "We appreciated the opportunity to meet with you . . . We can . . . I hope that when you have a project, you will call us." She delivered this with such presence that the group applauded—but it was a pyrrhic victory, because she missed an important step. After a few tips from her trainer she was able to say in future presentations: "We appreciated . . . May I ask if there is a project now or on the horizon we can look at . . . proposal?"

KNOW WHAT YOU WANT

The first step in closing is to know what it is you want to see happen at the conclusion of your presentation. The more specific you are in your *own mind* about the action you want, the more focused you will be about how you will ask for it, and the more likely it is you will get it.

Your close begins *before* you open—in your planning stage as you set your objective. Just as you prepare your summary by asking yourself, "What do I want clients to remember?", prepare for your close by asking yourself, "What is it I want the clients to do?"

Many salespeople in group-selling situations feel that their closes *fall flat*. They say they just can't get to the group and that they don't know what to say to them. This usually occurs for two reasons. First, they have not thought about the close in advance, or planned their objective and, therefore, are not prepared to ask for the next step or commitment from the group. Second, because they have not "checked" throughout the presentation and have little or no idea where they stand or, more importantly, where the clients stand, they feel awkward closing and initiating the action step, especially with a group.

One salesperson described himself as "always the brides- maid but never the bride." Although he made it to the finals, he lost far too many deals and attributed this to not knowing how to close. After observing him in a practice session his coach pointed out that 1) he hadn't planned out his close, 2) he did not ask for the next step, and 3) he did not check throughout his presentation. The coach asked him, "Well, what is it you wanted the last group (a group of diverse clients attending an educa- tional seminar) to do as a result of your presentation?" The presenter thought for a few seconds and said, "I wanted them to call me." Eureka! He found his close. It was that simple. He would suggest the next step. In his situation the next step was to position himself as a resource. Now he says, "Please call me . . . my card. . . ." Yet many salespeople forget to ask themselves, "What do I want the clients to do?" and then ask them to do it!

HOW TO CLOSE

To develop your close, ask yourself that simple question: *"What is it that I want the group to do at the end of the presentation?"* But remember the close isn't an isolated event. Therefore, checking throughout will set the ground work.

While you should be ready for a *yes,* with big-ticket decisions, it is unlikely that you will get a yes-or-no answer on the spot. Because multiple clients are present or the price is high and clients want to "huddle" after hearing you, clients will rarely make a firm decision about your product then and there. One salesperson said that in her 12 years of competing in "beauty contests," only once in Canada, did the clients (after giving approving eye signals to each other) say, "Okay, when can you start?" Since she did not expect a green light so early, she almost unraveled the sale by fumbling through an explanation of the roll-out steps. So if you get a "yes" on the spot you must be prepared with a roll-out or execution information. Always state the appropriate action step and say what you'd like to do. Then tell your clients you are confident you can do it.

Your closing step will vary based on the nature of the sales presentation you have given, the client's decision-making process, and whether you have been called in or if you initiated the idea. If you are selling to a large diverse group in a seminar sale where clients are there *to be educated* and the sales objective needs to appear secondary ("Client Seminars," Page 68), you might nonaggressively say, "I have a handout and folder. My card is in there. If you have any questions or would like to discuss any points, I'd be happy to speak with you. *Please call me.*" At the other extreme is, "When do we start?"

The less aggressive approach is more appropriate for a seminar selling situation to a large diverse group where you are positioning yourself as a resource. For example, if you are an investment banker presenting to a group of bank portfolio managers, inviting clients to call you would be appropriate. The other extreme, the *up and at 'em strategy* of *"Do we have a deal?"* is more appropriate for clients known for quick decision-making or when there is market-sensitive timing. Without crying "wolf," you should exploit time-sensitive situations that demand aggressiveness. For example, when you are dealing with a bureaucracy that traditionally prefers study to action, you can often *motivate action* by *conveying a sense of urgency* when a window of opportunity exists. You could say, "We know we have this opportunity *now* . . . in this market *now* . . . it may be a *long time* before we have an opportunity like this again to. . . . I'd like to begin the documentation today. . . . All I need is your go ahead (SILENCE)." You should be sure to capitalize on special opportunities in a particular deal, for example if a client can take advantage of a new or exceptional market condition.

It is *your job* to spark action by getting the clients enthusiastic and ready to act. Your enthusiasm, particularly in the close, is contagious—and can be a crucial factor in getting the client to move forward *with you.*

Between these alternatives, you can consider a *moderate but strong action step,* such as "We are confident about this and look forward to working with you. We are ready to proceed to the next step. All we need is your OK (SILENCE)." If you are making an introductory capabilities presentation, you might use the polite push of, "May I ask if at this time there is a specific project that we can look at now?" You can be even more low key with, "We understand what you are looking to achieve. We can and we would very much like to work with you." This close simply states your desire to work with the client. You might also close with a statement of your follow-up action, a benefit to the client, and an expression of your enthusiasm to do the deal: "I know you will be meeting." "I will call John on. . . ." We want to work with you because we know we can help you expand your market and increase branch revenues." "Thank you again for your consideration."

Being able to initiate the next step with confidence (close) is particularly important today. Products look more and more alike, tough competitors abound, situations are becoming more complex, and choices are becoming almost unlimited. Therefore, clients often are looking for more leadership. You may find that unless you are more assertive, someone else will close. This does not mean "hard sell," but it does suggest "serious sell" based on homework, dialogue, need satisfaction, and a call for action. The old "This is our recommendation," by reading the group, needs to give way to "This is our recommendation . . . *and we can begin today.*"

Determine the forcefulness of your close by your reading of the situation. But regardless of the intensity of the close, express your desire and ability to work with the client—ask for the business.

Some salespeople are natural closers, and natural closers keep closing in mind *throughout* their presentation. Born (or trained) closers look at closing as if it were a bull's eye. They work from the "outer rims" in toward the bull's eye to their objective to get the client to do X. They know their objective and are strategic and consistent in aiming at it, focusing and narrowing as they go. When a natural closer backs up from his or her target, it is only because he or she seeking a different path to it, consciously changes the target. Salespeople who have a problem closing do not possess this natural radar that seems to draw the closers in. While they, too, may begin on the outer rim, they do not aim toward the bull's eye, perhaps because they do not see it. Instead, they weave back and forth, without clear awareness of where they are and where they want to go. The incremental checking throughout the presentation is a way to help gauge present position and plan what the next step should be.

An example of how *not* to close was exhibited by a banker who made a sales presentation to ten banks on an excellent new stand-alone, foot in the door, microcomputer cash management product aimed toward the middle market customer. At the end of a one-day part-education and part-sales-training seminar that his bank offered to its correspondent bankers (Please see "Client Seminars," Page 68), the participating bankers were enthusiastic about this inexpensive, easy-to-demonstrate, *easy-to-sell and fast-to-close product*. They were ready to sign up. But then the hosting salesperson made a fatal error. Rather than closing on this one product, he made a "pitch" for the full array of cash-management products his bank could provide to the correspondent banks in the group. He went to the chalkboard and began to list each and every product—*all* of them. His "close" took 35 minutes and, by the end of it, all closing momentum was lost. *The participating bankers agreed to consider the "system"—* later. The opportunity to close on the spot was not seized. Six months later, not a single participant had signed up for the microcomputer product—and only four of the ten banks had even completed the paperwork.

What went wrong? This salesperson had strong relationships with each of the correspondent bankers, who knew and trusted him. He had an excellent product, which at that point had only one competitor. He had three success stories with major institutions who had provided testimonials. He even had a satisfied end user as a part of his presentation team who already had purchased the product from his bank. To top it off, he had an enthusiastic audience who needed his service in their market to generate fees and increase profits. The salesperson had everything going for him except one thing. He didn't have the slightest idea how to close! His minimal objective should have been to get the process going. He might have said, "I'm glad you all see the potential of this product . . . first step . . . let me go over the application . . . now. . . . once we do this . . . I will follow-up individually with each of you and your managers so we can start at our end. . . ." Everyone would have won. The bankers would have had a fee-generating product to sell to their customers and the salesperson could have launched his new product with a bang. This example shows that products—even unique, terrific products—don't sell themselves, and that almost *nothing* gets sold without closing.

Knowing the time to close deserves a brief mention. *Stopping* on time is as important as starting on time, especially with a group. If the group is about to have lunch or has other commitments, you will really lose points if you run over. Conversely, if the group is interested, they may request more time with you, so you should be prepared to accommodate the request. If there have been active discussions, you may even ask if it would be possible to continue, for example, for an additional 15 minutes. But you should not run over your allotted time without group agreement. A telecommunications salesperson lost a major contract because, as he laments, "I knew the group had to be out by 11:00, but we didn't finish until 11:30. With all other things fairly equal, those 30 minutes cost us the contract. The senior decision-maker was quoted as saying, "They knew I had to leave by 11:00. They just weren't sensitive to our needs!"

TO RECAP

- Check incrementally throughout your presentation to gauge client reactions and understand exactly how the clients are responding.

- Know what it is you want the clients to do and ask them to do it—ask for the business.
- Show enthusiasm.
- Keep track of your time.

The Group Selling Framework

Close

- Ask yourself before the presentation, "What do I want the clients to do at the end of the presentation?", and ask them to do it.

FOLLOW-UP

Your follow-up is very important. It offers an additional, simple way to differentiate yourself. Unless there are definite reasons why you should not follow-up, for example, if the client says to you, "I'll be working on this spin-off for the next week . . . so please give me a week. . . ." after a *final* presentation because a decision is imminent you should follow-up *the next day* with both a telephone call and letter. Your competitors probably will not be so conscientious.

FOLLOW-UP PROCESS

Let's look at the steps:

- Get your "thank you" *letters out by the next day* because timely letters give you an edge. Dictate the letter(s) within hours, not days, of making the presentation. Waiting several days will cost you the advantage.
- For *final* presentations with decisions pending, call your contact the next day before you finalize the draft of the letter. This call has three objectives: to thank him or her for the opportunity to present, to thank him or her for getting such a good group together, and to *ask if there are any other questions or concerns or if he or she needs additional information.* You will be amazed how many times this simple call will help *keep you in* or even *get you back in* the running. It will also give you insights as to what to touch on briefly on in your letter. For example, one consultant called his liaison after his presentation to learn the

client was concerned that the consultant "may not understand our market." In a telephone conversation and in two sentences in his short follow-up letter to the key decision-maker, the consultant was able to spell out his experience in that market and also to outline the kind of homework he would do to get to know the client's specific needs. He also touched on this point in his personalized thank you letter to the other clients.

One engineer making "the morning-after" call learned the client was about to go with his competitor. The client said, "Shawn, you're going to lose this one. Your quote was too high." The salesperson, confident in his product and price, said, "Thank you for the feedback. You know I work to get the best pricing as possible for you. May I ask what manufacturer they are using?" When the client named the same high-priced source he would have used, the engineer decided there probably was a pricing error on his competitor's part. In fact, his competitor had made an error and, when the client confirmed this with the competitor, Shawn got the contract.

• Follow-up letters can even be used to recover a fumble. One saleperson described a major presentation as a "disaster from a slow-start to an abrupt close." To make matters worse, he left one of his most important points out of the body of his presentation! He said he "just wasn't on" despite his preparation. To recover from this failure, he wrote short personalized letters to each of the fifteen committee members. Without apologizing or overselling, he simply communicated the missing point. Thanks to these letters he got the business.

• Alert your office to the fact that the client is in the *final* decision-making stage and tell key staff members how they can reach you if you are out so that you can answer last-minute client questions. For example, a salesperson answering her telephone at 5:10 p.m. saved a deal by convincing the client they were still interested. For the entire day she had been on another floor with product management preparing the implementation proposal; her secretary answered the client's calls all day with a, "She's not here. . . ."

Follow-up and follow-up letters show you are professional and have good business manners. They give you a chance to reinforce your understanding of client needs. They get your name in front of the client. They show the client you are indeed interested and on your toes. Most importantly, they are indicative of the level of future service you will provide.

"Leveraging seniors" can also be an important part of your follow-up strategy. When a company won a large contract, the sales team attributed "getting the ball across the line" to their chairman's call to the foreign company's president. His "How did the presentation go . . . we'd really like this piece of business" helped clinch the deal. Fortunately for this organization, there are still organizations whose senior management don't make themselves available. One frustrated account executive said, "We don't get support . . . X refused to mention we were calling on them about . . . When he was playing golf with their president. . . ."

Timely follow-up is very important in group selling situations especially when the client is about to make a decision and wants their hands held. *Therefore, increase your frequency of contact after you present.* Be sure to carry out any commitments you make to your clients, such as a promise to send them an article or to research a question. Follow-up—thank you letters, additional information, mailings, phone calls, visits, or tactfully leveraging senior management—can help you close.

Once you win the business, continue to "be there for the client." Unlike the cartoon drawing on the coffee mug that proclaims, "The sale begins after the customer says 'No!' ", the sale begins after the client says "Yes". Follow-up and follow-through help assure there will be *future* contracts and referrals. In today's highly competitive environment, your survival depends not only on gaining new clients but in getting add-on, repeat business and referrals. Two very good pieces of advice I got when I began selling were, "Stop selling and start helping," and "Save a little so that you can deliver more than you promise." Clients appreciate and reward you for both. So follow-up. Ask for feedback. Listen. Use what you learn. Stay on top of things. And make it a practice to *be there* and *deliver more* than you promise.

CLIENT SEMINARS

While the phenomenon of selling to a client group was devised by the clients, sales organizations themselves have created similar formats for selling to their clients. Many sales organizations host "client seminars," programs, where they invite clients from *different* organizations to attend their "educational" programs.

These seminars can range from a one-hour session to the four-day ski trip one company used to educate 100 of its clients. Since client seminars are gaining in popularity, let's look at how, with slight modifications, you can use the sales-presentation framework (opening, agenda/agenda check, need check, body, summary, Q&A, close, and follow-up) to make your client seminars more successful.

Client seminars and sales presentations to a client group consist of the same phases, but the emphasis changes. Let's look at the differences. First, the primary objective of a client seminar is educational, while sales is or should be an indirect objective. One client, after attending a seminar, complained to its brokerage house, "We are here to be educated. We know you and we know where you are! You went overboard on the sales pitch." Everyone, including this client, accepts that the organization hosting the client seminar has dual motives: 1) to provide an educational service and 2) to increase its business. Clients are more than willing to accept both of these motives as long as the selling motivation does not eclipse the educational one. But clients will often revolt when the "sales" blatantly overshadows "education." The second difference is that in a client seminar, the audience is usually made up of clients from *different* organizations and is larger, usually more than 20. And third, the amount of client participation generally is less than when selling to a group. On a sales continuum with one-on-one selling at one end of the spectrum and making a speech at the other end, group selling is midway between the two. Client seminars are about one-quarter farther down the continuum toward making a speech, and this usually means that client participation decreases. The group selling framework applies, but because of the larger size and greater diversity of the audience, and the primarily educational objectives of the seminar, client involvement and participation is generally less. In a client seminar your goal should be to have a minimum of 15 percent client participation. Again, the challenge is not to let it drop to be 5 percent or below!

Client-participation Continuum			
50/50%	70/30%	85/15%	95/5%
one-on-one selling	selling to a client group	client seminar	making a speech

Client seminars provide an excellent forum for selling, but many companies don't reap maximum benefit from their efforts. While the seminar agenda is usually well organized, the sequence of sessions are well planned, and the menus carefully chosen, the presenters/salespeople themselves often don't know how to work with a *diverse,* larger group of clients from *different* organizations. What could have been very successful turns into speeches which may, in part, satisfy the educational objective yet fall short of accomplishing the sales objective.

One presenter from a major investment bank who was knowledgeable, articulate, and personable in one-on-one situations got poor marks for the seminar on valuing fixed-rate, mortgage-backed securities he presented to 24 clients from major banks around the world. The room in which he was presenting was set up for 150 people. Instead of switching to a smaller room or requesting that participants move forward to create a small working group, he let them scatter about. He did not introduce himself (many presenters forget to do this). He walked in 15 minutes late without apologizing to the group. Furthermore, when he began his opening, did not create a reason why anyone would still be interested in mortgage-backed securities, especially in light of the current market. He did not give an overview of the agenda he planned to cover. Instead he engaged in a "Magical Mystery Tour," moving from topic to topic, with the audience never knowing what was coming next.

During the first 45 minutes of his one-hour talk, the presenter never checked if there were any questions or comments from the audience. He made assumptions with comments like, "Now that you feel comfortable with coupon spreads. . . ." He plowed through an esoteric subject without checking for understanding and questions. Not once did he ask, "Are there any questions?" Finally, a brave participant raised his hand and asked a question. But this did not inspire him to ask if there were any other questions, or even to ask if his answer indeed had satisfied the questioner. Although the slides he used were very well done and did help the audience follow his lecture, he used them nonstop in a dark room. Throughout his presentation he ignored the 20 computer screens bearing *his firm's name* encircling the room. Even when a second participant asked, "How can I get a handle on using models?", the presenter said, "I'm not here to sell our system. But we use X here." He missed a perfect opportunity to sell and educate at the same time. He could have said, "I'm not here to sell our system. As you may know we use X which was developed here in 1985 by. . . . It gives us. . . . Look at the screens. Our clients use it to . . . benefits. . . . Alternatives to this system are . . . systems (of course, he should not promote the strongest competitors). . . . We prefer this because . . . (benefits). . . . What questions . . . ?"

At the end, he gave no summary and, finally, he failed to close with an action step—not even "Please call me if you. . . ."

The dual objectives of this firm's seminar for its clients were to educate and to sell. All of these group selling errors not only interferred with the educational aspects, but they all but diminished the sales opportunities.

From maximizing the setting by orchestrating where people sit ("May I please ask you to move forward," "We are a small group . . . working together. . . ."), to checking whether there were any questions ("Before I move on, what questions. . . ?"), to closing with an action step ("Here are my cards . . . call me" or

"This is our department's structure. . . . you can call. . . ."). The presenter could have changed how this scenario played out and made the seminar more rewarding for everyone.

The opportunities in hosting a seminar for your clients are enormous. You get a captive, usually voluntary, audience from various segments of a market, drawn by the offer of a free or lower cost program. The mood is usually light and positive. Nevertheless, the seminar just opens the door; your client's business still must be earned. It is up to you to *follow-up* and pursue the business you have cultivated.

While these seminars are usually free for the audience (other than the time they invest), the hosting company has to pay to put them on in specialist's time, materials, facilities, luncheon, giveaways, and so on. On some occasions leading firms pay an "admission" as high as $10,000 to have their speakers present at a seminar. To maximize opportunities, salespeople need to recognize that a seminar held for a mix of clients, like selling to a client group, is new territory. The potential for business is there, but the salespeople need maps and tools to explore and exploit it.

SUMMARY OF GROUP
SELLING FRAMEWORK

The group-selling framework consists of:

- OPENING
- AGENDA/AGENDA CHECK
- CLIENT NEED CHECK
- BODY
- SUMMARY
- Q&A
- CLOSE
- FOLLOW-UP

The objective of each part of the group selling framework is to create a natural and comfortable give-and-take with the client group so you can be more responsive to their needs and set yourself apart from your competitors. The framework will give you a structure to use in developing your presentations and a process to fall back on during your presentation. At first you may feel self-conscious with the process, but as you use it, you will find that it provides a natural, logical flow that can guide and help you communicate more effectively.

The philosophy underlying the group selling framework is that the clients—their needs and situation, are the *center of the sale* and, as such, should be involved in it.

Now let's look in-depth at the *six group selling skills* you will use throughout the framework: presence, relating, questioning, listening, positioning, and checking.

DELIVERY—THE SIX CRITICAL GROUP SELLING SKILLS

INTRODUCTION

Your skills can make the difference between winning or losing a deal. What is it that causes a group of clients to respond to one salesperson's presentation and reject another's? With look-alike competitive products, it is not necessarily the product that make the difference. Some studies attribute up to 50 percent of persuasion ability to how the salesperson presents, 40 percent to his or her appearance, and only 10 percent to content. These statistics seem to say *what* a person says is far less important than *who* says it and *how* it is said. But form (who and how) and content (what) are not as distinct as they appear. What is discussed is only as valuable as the credibility assigned to it, and this is where *how* and *who* come into play. Mastering six critical group selling skills are the key to the *how,* and they can help *you be your best* and present your ideas in their *best* light. You can use them continuously throughout the framework to create give and take and make sure your story gets heard.

In group selling, it is how you communicate your product or idea as much as the product or idea itself that determines how clients respond to you. This is because, with everything else basically equal, people buy from people—people they have confidence in and *want* to do business with. In selling to a group, the level of scrutiny on the salesperson or the salesteam increases geometrically during the selling as collective judgment forms. The "you" element of your presentation is also more important today because products look alike to clients, and competitors are fairly equally matched in product and people. Finally, "big-ticket" items by definition create client caution: big dollars and careers are at stake! The old safety net of going with the "established, well-known provider" is no longer good enough. Today's managers are expected to and held accountable for making the right decisions.

By virtue of selling to a group, you place yourself on stage and that is where presence comes into play—stage presence. But to paraphrase noted poet, Archibald MacLeish, who cautioned poets to keep one foot in the book, but one foot in the world—keep one foot on the stage, but keep one foot in the audience. In today's client-centered environment the salesperson who gets up on the stage to preach to or educate clients will fall short of the salesperson who works *with* the clients. Clients who feel they are being spoken to in a condescending way, clients who do not feel involved, or clients who detect arrogance—whether they are dealing with insurance companies, hospitals, or investment banks—will find other salespeople to work with. Unfortunately, some salespeople confuse arrogance and confidence and lose business because they simply turn clients off. One salesperson who won a major contract in a tough competitive situation was told by the client, "You were the only group to directly address the objectives we sent to you and to ask for our ideas."

How you present your ideas will influence how clients respond to and evaluate them. Marshall McLuhan said over twenty years ago in a book of the same title, "the medium is the message." Nowhere does this principle hold truer than in group selling. For all intents and purposes as the salesperson you are the medium and, therefore, you are the message. The product is you. Presidential candidate Gary Hart tried as a part of his "comeback" after a scandal to dissociate his personal behavior (himself) from his message (his ideas). The failure of this strategy proved to the American public that the message and the messenger are one. Because an "audience" will not or cannot distinguish the idea or message from who presents it, it becomes clear that to be successful in group selling, you must present effectively. The client is thinking, "Is this the person I want next to me? Do I trust him/her?" Am I *comfortable* with them?"

How well you handle the client group is indicative to clients of how well you (and your organization) will perform both under normal situations and under fire. For today's demanding clients, when the sale involves an ongoing relationship, the salesperson becomes a personification of the product. Because clients have been stung by past disappointments, many demand the people who do the selling are the same people who will do the work!

All salespeople who can sell successfully one-on-one have the *potential* to sell successfully to a group of clients. What does it take? Group selling skills—six of them:

- *Presence*
- *Relating*
- *Questioning*
- *Listening/Observing*
- *Positioning of Ideas*
- *Checking*.

These six critical group selling skills have their roots in the critical one-on-one skills. But there are nuances to each of the one-on-one skills that need to be understood to maximize these high-stake situations.

Let's look at each of the six critical group selling skills:

PRESENCE

"Presence" or charisma is difficult to define, but it is readily felt. John F. Kennedy had it, and so did Dr. Martin Luther King and Franklin D. Roosevelt. They instinctively knew how to communicate to a group. They were able to keep a one-on-one kind of intimacy with thousands. They made each person in the audience feel like a Number One—and the only one. As they spoke, they brought the audience into their moment, into their present.

It is hard to believe that Franklin D. Roosevelt, the consummate presenter, was just "himself" when addressing the nation, but a recent rediscovery of the little-known "Roosevelt tapes" proves just that. While doing research at the Roosevelt library in Hyde Park, Robert J. C. Butlow stumbled across recordings made of Franklin D. Roosevelt in private conversations. On several occasions when his staff failed to turn off the device that taped his press conferences, the great communicator went about his business, apparently unaware that a recording machine was turning.

Until recently, only Butlow had heard these accidental recordings of Franklin D. Roosevelt's private persona. But in early 1988, a group of presidential scholars assembled to hear them. Their reviews, published in the *New York Times* (March 2, 1988), confirm that Roosevelt was Roosevelt on or off stage: "I was really quite struck by the degree to which the Roosevelt we know from the fireside chats is the Roosevelt of the oval office as well. I had that same buoyant, exuberant feeling listening to him." One scholar said it all: Roosevelt in private conversations could "hold the stage."

At the end of the article, one historian said Roosevelt's combination of "warmth and friendliness" was something that "some people may just be born with." The truth is that you *do* have to *be* born with it. The encouraging news is *we all* are born with it—not to the extent of a Roosevelt, but fortunately that level is not required to be extremely successful in selling to a group. Fortunately for most of us, the degree of "presence" and charisma needed to be a powerful speaker to hundreds far exceeds what it takes to sell to a group of 2 to 30 clients. As a matter of fact, any salesperson who can sell one-on-one can sell to a group. Unfortunately a considerable number of salespeople who are extremely good in one-on-one selling situations lose their presence; they freeze up when they appear before a group.

Lose what? I believe what they lose is their presence. Webster defines presence as "the fact or condition of being present: the state of being in one place and not elsewhere." As one best-selling book of the 1960s put it, *Be Here Now.* Salespeople who have no trouble "being there"—*being themselves*—in one-on-one situations often lose this quality of genuineness and comfort when they appear before a group. This thing called presence is captured in the description both salespeople and clients use to describe a great presentation—"I was *on*" or conversely, to describe a poor presentation—"I was *off.*" The keys to being "on" are 1) to be your one-on-one self (provided, of course, you are effective in one-on-one situations), 2) to be prepared, and 3) to have mastered the fundamentals and nuances of selling to a group.

Presence, while vital in one-on-one selling, is simply not as much an issue as it is in selling to a group. Facing a *group* seems to be the demon for most presenters. In response to their concern, they conclude, often subconsciously, that they have to be something other than who and how they normally are.

Salespeople who lose their presence are probably trying to be what and who they are not. *For the purpose of selling, let's define presence as being comfortable and confident with clients and making them comfortable with and confident in you.* A high degree of client comfort is necessary, especially for big-ticket items, since the decision-makers are in essence choosing a partner to stand beside them. They are placing their trust in you.

Some people have "presence" (stage presence) naturally. For those who get "thrown off" when facing a group, the first step in having "presence" with a group is to realize that your one-on-one self is your best bet. Once you understand this, you can do certain things to allow your one-on-one self to emerge. With this realization, preparation, and a retooling of your one-on-one skills (if you can sell one-on-one), you can be as effective in selling to a group.

One salesperson who needed to work on presence misdiagnosed his problem. He thought he needed to improve how he *organized* his presentations. But when he observed the video tape made of a practice presentation, he realized his eyes needed more work than his ideas! He was surprised to see that especially during the opening he looked at the floor and the walls more than he looked at the people. He also noticed that his voice was lifeless, except for the rare moment he looked at a client and spoke *to* him or her. This happened when he got questions from the group. As he responded to the questions, his real self jumped out. Last, but not least, he saw that he tended to get as far away from the group as possible. When taped in a one-on-one selling situation, none of the problems occurred. He decided to work on being more like his one-on-one self before working on anything else.

The problem of "presence" boils down to attitude and confidence. This can be seen with the client who scheduled a sales-training session with me. She was a New York City socialite who did fund-raising for a major museum. She said she was very effective in soliciting and getting contributions up to $5,000. Her problem was that she was unable to ask for contributions over $5,000. She wanted to learn how to ask for $6,000, then work her way to $20,000-plus.

This competent fund-raiser had created an arbitrary barrier in her own mind. While getting $20,000 could possibly mean different objections, benefits, questions, etc., fundamentally the only limit she had was the one she imposed on herself.

My job was to help the fund-raiser believe she could "multiply" her $5,000 skills into six figures. The Wizard of Oz had a similar task with the Lion, the Tin Man, and the Scarecrow. Each of us at one time or another can use a Wizard to help us defeat the witches we create for ourselves. When a wizard is not available, self talk can do the trick. Salespeople who are great one-on-one but fall apart with a group are like the socialite in that they create their own barriers. *The point is, if you can sell one-on-one, you can sell to a group.* Your natural self, preparation, and *a second tier of selling skills* are all you need.

Unfortunately, many salespeople abandon their one-on-one selves and, consequently, lose their presence. In addition to this, they don't prepare properly for a group and lack the *range* of selling skills they need. Their one-on-one skills are not enough; their skills need retooling. Rather than changing or adding to their skill set, they try to change themselves. They start to perform, but this does not work because most salespeople are not accomplished actors. Their "performance" is less effective than their "real" self. Nowhere was this more painfully obvious than in the 1987 Academy Award-winning movie *Broadcast News* when the brilliant investigative reporter was reduced to a puddle of nervous sweat in his once-in-a-lifetime chance as anchor. In his effort to apply the presentation skills he had been drilled on, such as "Emphasize one key word per sentence" and "Sit on the hem of your jacket to keep it from crumpling," he failed in the most important thing—to be himself. Hence he failed. The enormous talent he had demonstrated over and over again on tape as a field reporter vanished on the studio set when he tried to be someone other than who he was.

NERVOUSNESS

Nervousness or stage fright can be a real problem for salespeople selling to a group, depriving them of their presence. Fear of speaking in public (speaking to a group) ranks among the top three fears reported by most people. It can haunt and terrify salespeople not used to doing it. It usually attacks one or two spots in the anatomy, whether a weakened voice, trembling cold hands, a pounding heart, a dry throat, red cheeks, or an upset stomach. It becomes visible to clients in a lack of confidence or control. Famous performers from Sir John Gielgud to the popular singer Carly Simon report having bouts of extreme anxiety

before *every* performance. Since almost everyone—from professional actors to school children—is nervous speaking to a group,
it is not unnatural for you to be nervous when faced with selling
to a group. But nervousness can erode your presence if you don't
control it. When nervousness takes over it is like kryptonite on
Superman: it drains power, enthusiasm, zest, ease—and the
deal.

As has been said, most people get more nervous speaking *to*
a group than speaking one-on-one or one-on-two. While you
really can't eradicate nervousness, you can prevent it from
becoming debilitating. You can even make it work for you. The
ideas covered in this book can help reduce anxiety by guiding
you on the way you structure your sales presentation, prepare
for it, and deliver it. But perhaps more than anything else, it is
your ability to be your one-on-one self that can help quell
anxiety. Let's see how to do this.

HOW TO BE YOUR ONE-ON-ONE SELF

Let us look at the two main aspects of preserving your presence
by being your one-on-one self: Self talk and physical techniques.

Self Talk

Self talk is that inner talk you have with yourself. It can make
a big difference in how you cope with the prospect of selling to a
group. All people become anxious or nervous when they perceive
something as threatening. But this nervousness can be controlled or exacerbated by *what you say to yourself* and about
what is or is not going to happen.

What is it that you say to yourself that causes the feeling of
panic? Noted psychologist Dr. Albert Ellis, founder of the
Institute of Rational Emotive Therapy and author of *Guide to
Rational Living,* points out that people say something like this
to themselves: "Suppose I don't do well. I will meet with
failure/disapproval and *this would be terrible*." People who think
this way let their anxiety escalate to a "terrible" level and that
gets them into trouble. Looked at rationally, the "terrible" level

isn't justified. In most business situations, even if the worst-case scenario happened, it would not be the end of the world. It almost never would be truly terrible. Dr. Ellis' approach combats this by encouraging people to challenge the notion of "terrible". Instead, he suggests thinking about particular situations that did not work out or may not work out in the future as inconvenient or unfortunate, *but are not terrible*. This approach goes beyond semantics because the belief in "terrible" really leads to poor performance. When you as a speaker ask yourself, "What is the worst thing that can happen?", you probably will find that even at its worst a bad presentation will be a temporary setback, not a life-threatening situation. Unless you put the consequences in perspective, you risk "choking," and your anxiety will take over.

Dr. Ellis also has identified another inner message as a culprit: "I *should not* be nervous." In group selling, the stakes are high and, besides, you probably do not present to a group everyday. By telling yourself you "should not" be nervous, you only put more pressure on yourself and increase your anxiety. Instead, give yourself a break and say to yourself, "It's O.K. to be nervous." One salesperson not only accepted that he was nervous, he even tactfully mentioned it to his clients. He and his two teammates expected to meet with four individuals. They were led to a boardroom filled with 30 board members. He *used his nervous tension*. He said, "I did not expect to meet with all of you. Frankly, I am taken aback and genuinely impressed with the commitment this shows to. . . ."

Physical Techniques

Let's look at some simple physical techniques you can use:

Eye Contact
One of the best ways to evoke your one-on-one self in a group selling situation is to use your eyes as you do in a one-on-one situation. In the entire face no feature is more expressive than the eyes. Some specialists say that 80 percent of messages come through the eyes. Looking at one individual in the group at a time will trigger your natural communicating style. By talking

to someone rather than to the back wall or a sea of faces, you can put *life* and *expression* into your voice. Remember to look at one person as you begin and then one at a time. Protocol allows you to hold eye contact with each person for about five seconds. Believe it or not, this will help you feel more comfortable, and when you are comfortable, clients will sense this and become comfortable themselves. There is a second benefit to this: you will be forced to concentrate on someone else other than yourself and therefore you are likely to reduce your self-consciousness, and, in turn, your nervousness.

Since eye contact is important, do not wear heavily tinted glasses. Let your eyes communicate. They can smile and show you are genuine. Move your head back and forth without letting the movement become a distraction. Maintaining eye contact with all of the players will help you create a *group* atmosphere and will help you avoid engaging in a tête-à-tête that could turn your group presentation into a one-on-one. *Be sure to look at clients sitting to your immediate right and left since they are out of your line of vision and are easily ignored.* As you look at different members of the group, pay particular attention to the decision-maker. But do not focus on this person to the exclusion of others, since clients who feel ignored are likely to vote against you. Also, avoid getting lured into focusing too much on the client who nods approvingly (otherwise known as the Amen Corner). Even clients who are less enthusiastic can be won over by eye contact.

One salesperson learned the hard way how important paying attention to all players can be. He ignored the senior engineer, a strong influencer who was seated to the chairman's immediate right. When he asked the client what factors led to their choosing his competitor, the salesperson was told that they were "more comfortable with the *people side* of the competitor firm." While it may not have been the only factor, this unintended slight to a key decision-maker certainly did not help. A more experienced presenter, an advertising executive in a capabilities presentation, had better luck. When he failed to look to the far end where one department head was sitting so that she could identify her area and interest, his colleague interrupted and said, "Bob, I think you missed Sarah's division." This "save" by his colleague allowed Bob to apologize and turn to Sarah. Had she been ignored, her support may have been lost.

Finally, communication is a mirror. Looking at someone encourages that person to look at *you*. It says you are confident. It shows you are in control. It indicates you are interested in them.

Some of the pitfalls to watch out for regarding eye contract are:

- Begin by looking at one client—not the floor, ceiling, a sea of faces, or your nails/watch—as you begin.
- Pay more attention to the senior person and other key decision-makers, but *not* to the extent that you exclude, ignore, or offend influencers.
- Remember to look at the people to your immediate right and left who are usually out of your direct line of vision.
- Keep your head moving.
- Observe and use what is going on.

I know firsthand that eye contact and self talk work. Since over the past ten years I have become quite experienced in selling to groups, I rarely experience severe anxiety before I begin. However, I have much less experience in making speeches to very large audiences and, until recently, I found myself feeling extremely anxious in these situations. Invariably I would get off to a rocky start and my overall effectiveness would suffer. In an attempt to correct this, I asked a colleague to tape me practicing for an upcoming speech. The tape showed that in my "speech mode" I was not myself. I was trying to perform. I lost my energy and my commitment seemed to evaporate. The words were correct, but the impact was missing. So I practiced what I preached before we retaped: I did a breathing exercise and I looked into the eyes of one person as I began. This time there was a difference in my voice, in my enthusiasm, and in my clarity. I was talking to the audience, not reciting. So before each speech I say to myself, "It's OK to be nervous; be yourself." Then I breathe, look directly at one person, and begin.

Breathing

When you are anxious, your breathing can become irregular. You can help restore your natural breathing by breathing in and out deeply (do not sigh!) before you speak. A breathing exercise many salespeople find helpful for calming themselves down right before they begin is to breath *in* for a count of 6 (work your way to 10), hold for a count of 3 (work your way to 5), then exhale for a count of 6 (to 10), hold for a count of 3 (to 5), repeating at least three times. This kind of breathing is not natural, but it will help you get back to your natural breathing pattern. You can do this inconspicuously and naturally, especially if you practice in non-pressure situations. On your opening notes or materials, write the word B-R-E-A-T-H-E as a reminder. A few of these breaths will help calm you down. First of all, it will get your mind off your nervousness. Second, it will get your voice back to your natural level.

Overcome Physical Distance

Selling to a group has a physical dimension that simply is not an issue in one-on-one selling situations. Because there are more people to reach and the physical distance is greater, you have to project more than you do with one person: all eyes will be focused on you or, worse yet, not focused on you. Ordinarily, when you speak to someone one-on-one, the normal distance is about two feet (18 inches to 26 inches), but with a group the distance can be twelve feet or greater. Just this difference can create the feeling of being on stage. And because you need to reach several clients at one time, you have to project yourself as slightly larger than you normally do. Even with these challenges you will be most effective by keeping as close as possible to your normal one-on-one selling style (again providing it is effective), by projecting a bit farther through voice and body language and *by extending, not changing your style* while using the other six critical group selling skills.

Appearance

While appearance is not everything, in a group selling situation beauty is *not* only skin deep. Appearance is a part of presence and it can be indicative of what is going on inside the salesperson. Inappropriate appearance, along with bad timing and invisible visuals, cost a consulting firm its lion's share of a large training contract with one of the top ten banks in the world. Luckily, our firm had been offered a chance at a small piece of the business, so we were there when our competitor dropped the ball.

We were scheduled for an 8:00 evening presentation before 25 senior bank executives. Our presentation was to be an "add on" following an all-day presentation by our competitor. The executives were clearly tired after 10 hours of a preview by our competitor of the full curriculum, but they were accustomed to long days. Exhaustion was not their problem. We were still waiting to present when 8:30 rolled around. When we were invited in we couldn't believe our eyes.

The room was literally papered with tri-color flip chart sheets—inappropriate for such a group, since only a few of the 25 could read the small print. In fact, the consultant we learned periodically lost time throughout the day trying to retrieve information from particular flip chart pages which he couldn't decipher. But the worst part of the presentation was the appearance of the consultant, which was totally out of sync with his clients. While his clients were in shirts and ties, he was sporting a pair of WRANGLERS. They had made a small concession to informality by draping their suit jackets across the backs of their chairs, but not a tie was loosened. They were sitting straight, but he was leaning back in his chair. And as if to accent his insouciance, the consultant was drinking coffee (the only sign of sustenance in the room) from a folksy mug.

Everything was wrong with this "seat-of-the-pants" presentation, but it was the jeans that helped seal the presenter's doom and opened up our entrée to this major contract. The lesson is simple: Fit in.

Another consultant was too formal. The clients were at a ski resort and invited two firms to make half-hour presentations. Her competitor, while not wearing ski clothes, wore a tweed sports jacket, slacks, and a tie. She wore a navy suit, white shirt, and bow tie. She made her presentation as if they all were in an office building. Her "business-as-usual approach" when clearly the situation was not usual did not help win the client over.

One sales team, however, did everything right. Their "rah-rah" presentation was truly appreciated by the client, a leading university who awarded them the contract. Each of the ten slides displayed the school's logo, and four of the slides were of the beautiful campus itself and related to how they would address the school's objectives. All members of the sales team donned the school's colors, and two were alumni.

Appearance usually is an important part of presence. Without a doubt, there is a "show biz" aspect to presenting and the "on stage" aspect of group selling increases the importance of appearance. Therefore, give thought to what you wear based on where, when, and to whom you are presenting. In an East coast city, for example, you may choose to wear a white shirt or blouse and a navy suit. But in the West you may wish to wear taupe or grey—softer colors. One Atlantic Corridor real-estate broker arrived for his presentation in Denver clad in a navy suit, white shirt, and yellow polk-a-dot tie only to find himself seated in a room totally decorated in soft earth colors and among executives who blended right in! The point is, be yourself, but make sensible adjustments so that the client group can identify with you more easily. What you wear is only one small part of your fitting in, but it may be just the missing piece you need to get the deal. Just before you give your presentation, check your appearance.

Body Language

Body language is also a part of presence, so be aware of what yours says. Avoid negative body gestures, such as pointing at a client, folding your arms over your chest, or scowling when you are not happy about something. Remember your gestures get magnified when observed by a group, so avoid nervous behaviors: jingling change, tapping your fingers, demolishing paper clips, etc. These style-busters will not help and may well hurt your chances of winning the deal. Be aware of what your gestures could be saying about you. For example, bridging your finger tips together in a steeple formation as you are speaking shows you are "pontificating." Since this can come across as "holier than thou" to clients, it is better to avoid this gesture. On the other hand when a client does this, sit straight at attention and show you appreciate his or her expertise.

One of the worst things you can do is show horror on your face because of something your client or, worse, your teammate has said. One team of consultants lost a large contract because, according to the clients, the lead presenter's body language was disrespectful and rude to his own colleague. He not only interrupted his young legal associate, he actually grimaced as she spoke. The CFO had a daughter, an attorney in her early thirties, and was so offended by this that he awarded the contract to another firm that before the "beauty pageant" had been a definite "number two."

You should observe client body language—from where they sit to the expressions on their faces. Take note of where clients are sitting in relation to you. The client who selects the chair farthest away from you or directly opposite to you in the "lock-horns" position, may be telling you he or she is not a supporter. While you cannot draw conclusions from isolated behaviors, you can be alert to potential problems or opportunities. The client who chooses to sit farthest away from you may turn out to be the considerate smoker, and the client who does not look at you may indeed be concentrating on what you are saying but it is safer *not* to make assumptions.

Awareness will allow you to assess what is going on and figure out what to do. By reading and then testing signals, you can determine what, if any, adjustments need to be made, such as picking up or slowing your pace, skipping or adding material, checking and asking for feedback, using an individual's name (which happens to be great technique to break the ice with a "cold" client), or even changing how you position your idea.

Movement
As you present, move around and use gestures; don't stay glued to one spot. Use movement to heighten, not distract attention. For example, if you are standing, you can move to the left or right to address particular clients, or you can move forward and then backward to accentuate points. Move in a way that makes you appear confident, and when appropriate, relate your movements to your points.

You can use your hands to capture and hold attention. With your fingers tick off points (first, second, and so on), or tap the table to show determination. If you are using visuals, free yourself to move about by placing your pen on the overhead to point to a line. When you are seated you can get up and refer to a visual, then return to your seat. If you are sitting, inch up in your chair when you talk about price. This will show you are confident, but sit back slightly when a client objects to give him or her room and indicate you are open to the feedback.

Voice

Your voice is a factor in your presence. It reveals your comfort level, your confidence, your commitment, and more.

Having *life* in your voice is important. It keeps the presentation interesting and alive and it gives you credibility. As mentioned, *do not read to clients*. Most people, other than professional actors, lose feeling when they read. Words that come from inside, not off the paper, and are directed to someone eye to eye, are usually infused with feeling. Words off paper can sound wooden. Even words you write one hour before are "past tense," and it usually takes the talent of a professional actor to summon up the experience, re-enter it, and inject it with life. Salespeople who read to clients often justify this by saying that otherwise they might forget something or say it imperfectly. But unless you are reading figures, presenting new complex information, or technical facts that must be exact, the perfection you gain by reading won't matter. Your clients may be so bored they will forget what you say anyway. Also, don't memorize word for word what you plan to say since, as with reading, your words are apt to sound wooden. You should, of course, refer to your proposal preferably to help keep your thoughts flowing.

At worst, your voice should be a non-issue; at best, it should be persuasive. While commitment in your voice is first and foremost, you should pay attention to volume, pace, expressiveness, and enunciation. A high-pitched voice can be annoying to listeners. Men have an advantage because their voices are lower by nature. Women should not try to sound like men, of course. But women with high-pitched voices can find their natural pitch. This process of "opening up the throat" which happens when you yawn, may require a few voice lessons. To get your voice at its best speaking level (and to reduce nervousness), try this exercise: breath in slowly as you count to ten, hold for count of five, then breathe out slowly for a count of ten, hold for five. Repeat several times. Practice doing this daily and right before you begin.

As for *volume,* the size of the group you are addressing and its physical distance from you will tell you how much to project your voice. For small groups of three or four clients, your natural speaking voice will do. For larger groups up to 25, you probably will not need a microphone unless the room is very large, for example, in a huge boardroom equipped with mikes. You can speak louder or lower your voice to a whisper to add emphasis and help get your message across. But when you soften or raise your voice to make a point, remember to return to your normal volume! Parenthetically, if you need to use a microphone, use a lavaliere microphone when available since it will give you more physical freedom. If you are using a stationary microphone, remember to speak about one-half inch *over* the top of it, not directly into it. As with all equipment, test it before you present.

Articulation is more important than sheer volume, so speak clearly. Pronounce your r's, ing's, etc. While colloquial pronunciations are certainly acceptable and often preferred, dropping of g's in ing's is generally considered a sign of untidy speech. How you pronounce proper names also matters. If you are selling in Des Moines and you pronounce the "s," the client will know how little you know about the area. To evaluate the expressiveness of your voice, tape yourself, then listen objectively for variability in your voice. Again, look at someone as you speak to add life to your voice.

Keep your *pace* lively. The old "go slow" adage couldn't be more off-base. Research shows that people who speak more quickly (not rapid fire) are often viewed as more intelligent than slow speakers. *Nothing* but *nothing* is worse than a presentation that plods or lumbers along. Vary your pace and use pauses to show significance of certain words.

While you must keep the pace going, you should take advantage of pauses. For example after you cover a main point, wait a second and look at clients. This pause will give them a chance to react, nod their heads, show a quizzical look, or speak up and give you the chance to respond.

After stating a key word, pause *after* the word for emphasis, not before it. The French impressionist Paul Cézanne always left a small piece of canvas unpainted. When you are selling to a group you must paint a picture. In the tradition of Cézanne, leave a space or two for silence.

Choice of words is also important in maintaining your presence. Don't trivialize a point by being repetitious or using slang. Don't overuse a word or try to be cute. One presenter used the word "grumpy" to describe the Federal Government's reaction to their exploitation of a loophole. At first, the use of the word was effective, but by the fifth time he used it, the group no longer found it amusing; it lost its appeal and actually diminished the seriousness of his message.

Be Yourself
Presence is hard to define, but it is easy to spot. To have presence, be confident in yourself and be yourself. The best way to project "presence" is to be yourself with confidence and openness. To get a picture of how you really come across, you can be video taped followed by a critique of the tape for eye contact, appearance, voice and body language, etc. (Please see "Physical Techniques," Page 82.) Doing this with a trainer or coach can be invaluable.

RELATING

INTRODUCTION

One of the advantages of selling to a group is that you get the opportunity to meet and influence key decision-makers—all at one time. But to take advantage of this, you first have the task of establishing rapport with them *as a group.*

With everything else equal, it is easier to build rapport with one person at a time than with a group. The potential for natural "intimacy" is far greater in one-on-one selling situations than in group selling situations, where forces like physical distance, multiple people with multiple needs, a more structured setting and time frame, and the pressure of an impending decision are operative. In addition to having to face several individuals, each with his or her own needs, you also have to "get" with the group as a whole. This is a challenge since the group can develop a personality all of its own. Selling to a group not only takes more skill, it takes greater *sensitivity.* It requires being more selective in what you say, how you say it, and what you do not say. A phrase that is an easy toss-away in a one-on-one situation can cause irreparable harm "in public."

While good chemistry can happen naturally, more often than not, it must be earned. Good chemistry can be fostered by knowing as much as possible about each group member before the meeting, building rapport during the presentation, and showing you can add value.

HOMEWORK

Homework on all members of the client decision-making team is the first step to understanding them. You can do research by networking your own organization as well as in the client's organization. Once you understand the hot buttons and needs of each group member, you will be able to position your ideas so that they match up with the client's needs.

Ideally you would have met each client decision-maker *before* your sales presentation. One-on-one pre-meetings are helpful in building rapport and ironing out potential problems *before* the presentation. But the ideal is not always possible and because of time, distance, or corporate structure, you may not be able to get to any or all players. When you cannot reach them directly, you can do in-depth homework on the individuals you were unable to meet prior to the presentation.

You and your team should know *who is who, who pulls the strings, who knows what, who is influenced by whom, who feels what,* and *which subjects you should or should not bring up.* Client knowledge is critical to your success because it will enable you to bring relevant ideas and it increases your sense of comfort with the clients. Conversely, it will help make clients comfortable with you. When you do not feel comfortable, clients can sense it and psychologically pull away from you. But when you are comfortable, you will be able to create a comfort level among them. (Please see "Preparation," Page 129)

Building Rapport during the Presentation

You can establish rapport or erode it throughout your presentation by *how* you present your ideas. With each sentence you can build a bridge or erect a wall. Throughout the sales presentation framework there are many opportunities to build rapport: in your *opening* you can acknowledge the individuals who helped prepare you for the meeting without being obsequious—"Over the past two weeks I have met with Bill and Tom . . . operations . . . very helpful. . . ." In the body, you can refer to a particular interest someone has—"Tom pointed out the concern for. . . . We have. . . ." You can thank the client for bringing up a particular point. By your *need check* you can demonstrate you are interested in the clients' concerns. When you respond to *objections* you can establish yourself as straightforward, knowledgeable, and non-defensive. When you *answer questions* you can do so with sensitivity so that you encourage and satisfy the questioner. You can considerately *check* to make sure your answer addressed the concern. With your *body language*—your eyes in particular—you can include everyone and make them comfortable. In describing the client's situation or your ideas, you can *choose words that are non-judgmental.*

One investment banker failed to do this and said, "The one thing I'm sure you are dreading is going back to the state with your hat in hand each year for. . . . It certainly won't look good for you." His accusatory tone throughout the presentation had made the group uncomfortable but this "hat in hand" zinger made everyone squirm! Although he was right, his callous portrayal of the situation—*worse yet in a group setting*—cost him the deal. Another consultant lost a contract because he kept referring to the "mess" at the client's company. The chairman finally said, "Frankly, we are aware things are not good, but we think of the situation as *challenging*." While the chairman had already used the word "challenging" several times to describe the situation, the salesperson missed the message.

Everything that you do and say, from checking if your agenda meets the group's expectations to asking continuously whether the group has any questions, will help you build rapport and establish yourself as someone the clients want to work with. The thing to keep in mind is that people buy from people, not companies. If they do not like you, they will figure out a way to do it away from you. Rapport with the clients is in almost all situations a prerequisite to doing business. Let's look at some communication techniques to help you establish rapport.

USING CLIENTS' NAMES

Even if a client tries to thwart your efforts to build rapport, it is your responsibility to work to improve the situation. If someone is closed off, with eyes down and arms folded, a simple gesture such as using the client's name—"As Jim mentioned earlier, this is the critical question." —can warm up a cold situation. But be sensitive not to overuse a name, as one executive did on an interview on "Wall Street Week." Literally every response he made began with "Lou."

EYE CONTACT

Eye contact will help create rapport with clients. One salesperson describes how a manager walked in five minutes late, sat down, and for 20 minutes did not look up. The salesperson *made a point* to look frequently to the spot where this client was sitting and addressed comments to him along with the others as if he were involved. Gradually, the manager began to look at the salesperson. Forty minutes into the presentation he was making supportive comments and by the end of the presentation he was won over. Continuing to look at someone who is not responsive and does not return the gesture requires discipline and guts. It is much easier to "play" to the Amen Corner where clients nod approvingly.

HUMOR

Humor at the right moment can also be a way to build rapport. The president and two of his senior people from an insurance company were meeting with the CEO, CFO, and the risk manager of a Fortune 100 company. After the president of the insurance company opened he asked the clients to tell them about their situation and their concerns about director liability. After the clients spoke for about a half hour, the CEO said to the president, "You are the first group who asked about our worries and issues before telling us what we need." The president modestly and in a jovial tone replied, "It has taken us a *long* time to figure this out, but our clients *really do know* more about their business than we do." Everyone chuckled and the meeting progressed. Within two months this insurance company, a leader in its field in market share and profitability, added another new client to its list.

RAPPORT KILLERS

Not all rapport problems stem from the client. One sure way to kill rapport is to offend the client. The CFO from a savings and loan challenged the valuation of his branches made by the presenting investment bank. He said, "These numbers are simply too low." The vice president from the investment bank turned to his colleague, an associate, to respond to the CFO's complaint. Although the associate was about 25 years younger than the CFO and admitted feeling uncomfortable using the CFO's first name, he said to the CFO and other members of the executive team, "No, I think the numbers are right, Michael." The CFO then demanded, "Well, how did you get your figures?" When the associate gave him the breakdowns, the CFO could only shrug. Even if the associate did succeed in convincing the bank executives his numbers were right, he damaged the relationship by offending face. Not surprisingly several weeks after the meeting, the bank pulled out of this billion dollar deal.

The associate could have used the CFO's objection to build rapport, get a dialogue going, and help cement the deal. Even if the CFO's colleagues had not been in the room, this blunt approach would have been inappropriate. But in the presence of others, it was downright destructive. The CFO lost face and the investment bank lost the deal. The outcome may have been quite different had the associate said, "I know you want to use the most favorable figures and so do we. That is a fair question (empathy). May I ask what you are thinking in saying they are low? . . . ." to get the CFO to explain what he was basing his opinion on and what numbers he would have used. In mergers and acquisitions, almost nothing is as important as the people side of the deal in getting it to work. Not surprisingly, this anti-relationship approach cost them the deal.

Another example of how a salesperson can be his or her own worst enemy was recounted by a partner in an advertising firm. He had been meeting in a well-appointed room at his agency with six clients, consisting of a CEO and five members of his senior team. The room they were in was a bit too small for the large group, and the CEO mentioned twice that the room was warm. At break time the partner suggested to the account executive newly assigned to this client that she move the group to the other conference room, a less elaborately decorated room but one that would be larger and cooler. By way of background, throughout the morning there had been a slight tension between the account executive and the CEO, whom she considered to be a chauvinist. The account executive suggested they switch rooms and as the CEO entered he said, "Well, this is a lot better." The account executive responded, "Are you being sarcastic?" Her inappropriate, defensive comment had a deadening effect on the second half of the meeting. The partner later said that "It took a full half hour to take the chill out of the air. I switched account executives but we didn't get that piece of business." The partner had read the client's comment differently; he thought the client was trying to be friendly. But even if the account executive were right in interpreting the CEO's intent, her response was inappropriate. She would have been much wiser to let the remark go unanswered, or better yet, to agree! If she were concerned about using a room normally designated for internal meetings, she could have checked: "We may be more comfortable in here. Will this be O.K.?"

Another way to destroy rapport is to allow a "show down" to take place in a group setting. Clients who take a position publicly are reluctant to back down from it. So too, if it looks like a flat *no* is about to come your way, find a way to postpone this so that you can regroup.

Simply stated, if you can't establish rapport with clients, you won't be able to sell to them. Relationships are very important, even in today's transactional environment. It is relationships that make transactions happen with any regularity and you usually need a relationship to do a transaction.

Being able to relate to clients begins with understanding them: knowing how they think, what they need, and what will make them look good. Essential to rapport is respect for clients, an appreciation that their needs are different, the belief, as the old saying goes, that they (customers) are always right, and a feeling of genuinely liking them. You can at least usually neutralize a hostile client group if they sense you are genuine and interested in them. Rapport is the first step in developing a relationship. It can lead to trust and trust leads to business.

QUESTIONING

The cost of *not* questioning is too high. You won't be able to sell to a group if you don't ask and answer questions. While questions are an essential and challenging part of one-on-one selling, they are more important and even more difficult to deal with in a group setting. Whether the questions are from the clients to you or from you to the clients, they create all-important interaction. Questions from clients not only enable you to satisfy client concerns, they give you an opportunity to build credibility because you can handle them spontaneously. Questions from you to your clients will help them associate *you* with an interest in them and will afford you vital feedback and insights into what and how they are thinking.

ENCOURAGING QUESTIONS

Make it a point to invite clients to ask questions *throughout* your presentation. You are not making a speech; you are selling to a group. Don't rely solely on the Q&A as the place to catch client questions. Let clients breathe life into your presentation. Of course, clients will sit back if you let them. Because their colleagues (juniors or seniors) are present, *clients too may feel uncomfortable* and inhibited about asking questions. They don't want to appear "stupid" or uninformed, and therefore, are more likely to be less talkative than they might be in a one-on-one situation. To involve them, you must encourage them to ask questions as they occur to them. Simply say, before you move into the body of your presentation, "Please ask questions or make comments as we go along," and then remember to check with "Do you have any questions?" as you go along. You will need to continue to ask if clients have questions because a single invitation such as "Please ask questions as we go along," lasts only so long and it will not work like a flu shot.

Some salespeople resist encouraging such interaction. I think this is because they confuse group selling with making a speech. Speech protocol requires that you keep questions to a minimum until the Q&A, because a speech, typically made to a large, often incohesive group, needs rhetorical unity. If you as a speechmaker tried to accommodate a large number of random questions from the audience as you presented, you would likely end up with a disjointed presentation. Therefore, speechmakers typically view questions *during* their speeches as interruptions that have to be controlled and they often look upon questioners as "hecklers."

But in selling to a group, questions are anything *but* interruptions. They are integral to the group *selling* process. Since the clients are typically smaller, unified groups, questions from them allow you to position your ideas to match up with their needs. Some salespeople are also hesitant to invite questions *during* their presentations because they feel they will lose control. Quite the contrary, questions can help *you* stay in control through an improved presentation, *if* you know how to handle them: not to over answer them, when to answer them, and how and when to *table* them.

Of course, there may be rare situations in which you may not wish to encourage client questions during the body of your presentation. For example, if a client is *very* talkative or if you have a very short amount of time to present, you will wish to reserve questions for the Q&A period. Nevertheless, the more clients are involved and are a part of the solution, the greater the likelihood you will close.

RESPONDING TO CLIENT QUESTIONS

When a client asks you a question in a group setting, whether during the question-and-answer period or before, there are several considerations to keep in mind, again, because a group is present.

GUIDELINES

Here are some guidelines:

• *Listen.* Do not interrupt. Listen with your mind and eyes. Be prepared to use what you hear. Listen to the complete question. Even if the client asks the same question twice, there may be a word change that can give you more insight into what the client needs.

• *Avoid defensiveness.* Becoming defensive will work against you in one-on-one selling situations but it is even more of a problem in group selling situations. If you lose your cool publicly, make the client feel uncomfortable in front of his or her colleagues, or "take on" a member of the client group, you will almost invariably lose. It is the classic case of "winning the battle" but "losing the war."

Even if the question from the client has a critical tone to it or corrects or challenges you, do not become defensive. Defensiveness on your part will only close down communications and cause you and the client to lose face. One investment banker was asked by one of the clients in the group if he thought his close relationship with their major competitor would be a conflict of interest. The client said, "How can we trust you if you are so close with X?". The investment banker said the comment "struck deep." He was offended because he felt his integrity was being challenged. Instead of becoming defensive, he took a breath and looked at the question from the client's point of view. His mind flashed to headlines of insider trading and the bias it created among clients against the "Street." He responded, "Many clients would not be so frank. And I appreciate the chance to respond. Have I ever done or said anything to indicate that I or our firm . . . hold our discussion in utmost confidence. . . . I think I could, by my depth of knowledge of the industry, be of value to both of you *without* hurting either of you. . . ."

The investment banker realized by this question that he had quite a way to go to win the trust of this client and that it was unlikely he would get the piece of business under discussion. While he knew he had not satisfied the concern there and then he did begin to address it. He then began a program of frequent calling at multiple levels to establish the trust he needed.

• *Don't devalue questions.* Be careful not to devalue the question inadvertently or intentionally with a response like, "No, that's really not valid because. . . ." or "Well, you *may* have a point there, *but*. . . ." or "No, that's not correct." Comments like these will diminish the question and are likely to alienate, offend, or embarrass the questioner in front of others in the group.

• *Don't over answer.* Listen to the question and address the client's specific question. Avoid the temptation to give additional information that is not directly related to the question unless there is a pressing reason to do so. The point to keep in mind is that others are present and if you give a long, contorted answer you risk losing the interest of the other players. Remember, the questioner is not the only game in town, you are in a group. Also, if you do not know when to stop, you may talk yourself out of business.

• *Don't repeat strong negative words.* If the question has an inflammatory, provocative, hostile word such as "churning" or "unethical," most of the time you should *not* repeat the word itself since it will reinforce it. Instead, say, "I can understand your concern. What specifically . . . ?" For example, when a top firm advised the client of its half a million dollar "hello fee," the client's chief advisor said, "We are *deeply offended* by your request for a half million up front." The senior banker on the account cringed when a young vice president replied, "I can understand you would find this *deeply offensive,* but I hope you can live with it." With this retort sparks started to fly. It would have been much more effective for the vice president to delete the word "offensive" from his reply and to eliminate the "take-it-or-leave-it" tone of his response. He might have said, "I can understand your concern. May I ask why you feel that way?" And then after listening to the client the vice president might have said, "Because of the number of hours we rack up so easily and the resources we put on . . ., I would appreciate it if you could agree with the fee so we can proceed on your behalf."

• *Check by asking, "Does that answer your question?"* Once you have answered the question, ask, "Does that answer your question?" to give you the feedback you need to determine if you have satisfied the question or if you need to discuss it further. In this way you can avoid over answering and still make sure you have satisfied the concern.

- *Make sure there are no other questions.* Do not assume that once you get one question it is the only question. Ask, "Are there any other questions?"
- *Use questions to score points.* You can use questions from the client to help you score points. As you answer questions, answer them accurately to satisfy the question without becoming long-winded. Capitalize on the opportunity to "load" your answers with your selling points but do so tactfully. For example, if a client says, "How many people are assigned to a project our size?", you could say, "Four." But you could score points by saying (especially if a power base player has asked the question), "I know our team is the key to the success of this. Based on the scope of what we have discussed, we think a team of four people . . . so that you get. . . . The team I have in mind consists of me and (possible names, experience level, and team structure). You may have read about X in. . . . Does that answer your question about our team?"
- *Avoid exaggeration, but don't sell yourself short.* Your answers will give clients a feel for your depth and confidence. While you do not want to oversell or promise more than you can deliver, you also do not want to sell yourself short. While you should be scrupulously honest, be sure to give the full picture. Sometimes a simple answer to a question might not tell the full story. For example, during an important presentation, a client asked the salesperson, "Will your reporting system give us X information?" The salesperson said, "No." *He answered the client's question but he missed the client's concern.* In doing so, he missed an opportunity to sell his idea. Had he asked the client, "I know it's important for you to get specific information. Can you tell me exactly what you are looking for in wanting X number?", he would have realized that his system, while it could not give X number, could easily provide the client with the information he needed.
- *Narrow down broad questions/Find out what's really on the client's mind.* It has been said, "Don't answer a question with a question," but very often you will need to ask a question to be able to provide an answer that gives the client the information he or she is really looking for. Since it can seem presumptuous or impertinent to respond to a question with a question, *preface* your question with a empathetic comment. If a client says, "How does the offshore tax . . . ?" You probably need more information

about what the client wants to know so that you can position your response. You should give first by saying something like, "Yes, I know that offshore tax . . . is important." Then you should seek clarification by asking, "May I ask what specific aspects are of concern to you?" In this way you can better "read" the client's mind. Prefacing the question with a comment like "Yes, I can see that would be a concern. *So that I can focus on the specific . . . ?*" will *soften* the question and make the client willing to point you in the right direction. If you don't narrow down the question, you risk falling into answering the wrong question or presenting your answer from the wrong perspective.

• *Be prepared for questions.* You will have to be, as the expression goes, "fast on your feet." But most salespeople who are "resourceful" and can "dance" really are well-prepared and have solid experience. Be fully grounded in your subject. You need depth of information that exceeds what is in your proposal. This is especially important for answering questions the clients bring up. Homework and experience will help you anticipate and prepare for clients' questions. If you lack depth in a particular area you should include a specialist in your team who will have the expertise you will need. One U.S. sales team that anticipated needing up-to-the-minute market information alerted a specialist in Switzerland so that he would be available during their presentation for a multimillion dollar deal. Having lined up the information and resources helped close the deal. Newer salespeople in particular should meet with their managers and specialists to discuss common tough questions so that they will be prepared to satisfy questions.

• *Table it.* Sometimes you will have to table questions during the body of your presentation. For example, if you are asked a question that would be better addressed later in your presentation after you cover preliminary information, you can usually *table* the question with a simple comment like, "If it is alright with you, I'd like to hold that for a few minutes because it is important and I want to cover it in the context of. . . ." This is perfectly acceptable in almost all situations. The only time you should go ahead and deal with something that ideally would fit later is a question from a senior executive. For example, if the CEO raises the point about tax liability, *address it, then and there,* at least in part, since executives are not accustomed to being put on hold. If you *must* cover other information first, say, "I will cover . . . and tax liability" but, at a minimum, bullet the key tax points you will be covering.

• *Be accurate/get back to the client when necessary.* Since sales presentations are often conclusive (the client will be making a decision soon after the presentation) it is important to have the answers to the questions clients ask; however, if you do not have the answer, do not jeopardize your credibility. Find out exactly what the client needs to know, say you would like to do more/some research, and set a time to get back to the client.

• *Think first.* When you get a question from a client, it can be helpful to take several seconds to contemplate the question before answering. Fast is not always smart. Making it apparent you are giving the question thought can be flattering to the client, since it shows that his or her question is thought-provoking. A reflective moment for some questions, without sounding like Detective Columbo, can add to your credibility. It will also improve the quality of your response. The president of a Fortune 100 company says he thinks up "off-beat" questions, ones the salesperson probably has not heard before, so that he can observe how the salesperson approaches the question. He says that he is wary of people who answer these questions too quickly.

• *Recognize questions that are really objections.* Although you can never really be 100 percent sure what a client's intent is in his or her comments or questions, it is often possible to read between the lines to detect signs of hostility. While many questions are fundamentally what they appear to be, some questions mask hostility and are objections in disguise. Such questions may be overtly hostile such as, "How much are you going to hold us up for this?" Some may be less overt—"Has the meter started ticking?" Under all circumstances it is important not to become hostile in return. Rather than take offense, try to understand the feeling as well as the content of the question. The way to do this is to *get more information* from the client, and observe the client's body language and tone of voice. You cannot read someone's mind but you very often can read their body gestures and tone. You can also read patterns. Quite often the *first* question from a client in the group will be, if there is going to be one, the "loaded" question which is aimed to "get" you. This question is usually asked by the client who opposes you, the change you represent, or both.

A question that comes up sooner or later in most presentations is, "What experience do you have with situations like ours or in our industry?" This is a perfectly legitimate question. But if it is the *first* question—especially if you or your institution are still on an experience curve—it could be raised to "put you in your place" as the new kid on the block. The way the question is delivered (friendly vs. unfriendly) will be indicative too. For example, if the client asking the question is scowling, has his or her arms crossed, or sits farthest from you, you might draw the conclusion that this question is being asked to discredit you.

A red flag should go up in your mind if the first question is asked by the client seated farthest from you and to your immediate right (seat of honor) of the client decision-maker. In one such case, without any signal of emotion, a "right-hand" client asked as the first question, "Do you have an office here?" The presentation was being made by a U.S. company in a foreign country where nationalism was an issue and the presenting company did not have a branch. Before going in, the sales team knew this was a decided weakness since its competitor had a local branch office. The "question" from the client was really an objection—a major objection. When a question like this is not handled right, the likelihood of getting the business is nil.

The salesperson replied, "We do not at this time. However, we will be opening three offices over the next two years and we are seriously looking at this market, since we have done extensive work with X and Y here over the past five years." His response was brief and clear. It was non-defensive. *It was also totally ineffective.* The salesperson responded to the question as if it were a question that could be addressed by a yes or no answer. He responded to the content of the question but completely ignored the feeling. The client got what he wanted—a point to score *against* the salesperson's team: No office. As one excellent salesperson said to his junior people, "When we go into a sales presentation, we and our main competitors all go inequal. We all have 100 points going in and the clients around the table are there to subtract points, not add them on. The firm with the most points left at the end of the presentation gets the business—almost always."

When the salesperson answered the question about the office he lost a lot of points. With more homework, skill and sensitivity to the political implications, he might have at least held the line. The salesperson could have benefited from using the consultative process to address the concern. By listening to what the client was looking for, the salesperson could have shown he was interested in what the client needed and he could have addressed those specific needs. He could have said, "Certainly, I appreciate your question. At this time we do not have an office. *May I ask what specific things you would be looking for in our having a branch here?*" Instead, he gave a generic answer he could have given to any of a dozen clients. Worse yet, had the salesperson done his homework he would have known that his new parent company did have a subsidiary there. But even without this "ace," he could have dealt with the question more effectively than he did. Had he gotten the client to open up he could have addressed availability, the foreign exchange problem, commitment to the region, and the driving issue of nationalism. Two weeks later he learned he did not get the deal because of "availability." Four face-to-face calls involving international travel, numerous telephone calls, and more than one and one half years of prospecting and follow-up went down the drain.

Many people think using a question to get specific information about the client's question will open a Pandora's box of problems. On the contrary, it will prevent you from playing right into a gunslinger's hands. It will 99.9 percent of the time help you provide the client with the information he or she really needs. It is up to you to use questions to hold the line and score points. First of all, most objection-type questions are broad. Secondly, the client already has a perception and rather than go out on a limb to figure out what the client is driving at, you can get insight into that perception and deal with it.

• *Use eye contact to keep the group involved.* When you get a question from a client in the group, you have the challenge of keeping the other group members interested as you answer. Even though one person has asked the question, your response must be addressed to all members of the group. Of course you should direct about 50 percent to 70 percent of your reply to the client who asked the question, but you should include everyone else at least 30 percent of the time. However, when one of the key power-based decision-making clients asks a question, you should address about

85 percent of your answer to him or her. You can address the group by making eye contact with the other group members as you answer the question posed by one client. If you direct your answer exclusively to the client who raised the question, your presentation could evolve into a one-on-one and you could risk losing the interest and attention of the other client decision-makers. Begin your answer by looking at the person who asked the question, but then look at the other clients, too. As you conclude your answer, be sure you are focused back on the client who asked the question and check with him or her by asking, "Does that answer your question?" By looking at others too while you respond, you can take the pressure off the questioner so he or she does not feel obliged to prolong the discussion or ask a follow-up question.

• Give clients time to answer the questions you ask. Once you ask a question, develop a sense of timing so that you can strike a balance between giving people enough time to answer without creating a period of silence that makes them uncomfortable. Usually, don't let more than about six or so seconds to pass as you wait before you say, "Fine, let's move on." Look at clients with your head straight, not tilted to encourage clients to answer or ask questions. Silently wait about three to six seconds and listen for questions to come your way. Your demeanor will tell the clients that you expect and welcome questions from them. (Please see "Eye Contact," Page 95.)

TO RECAP

How you handle client questions and how well you ask questions are critical to your success. If you turn off even one key player or influencer, it can cost you the business.

Questions from clients create an opportunity for spontaneity, and, therefore, give you an opportunity to distinguish yourself, your idea, and your organization. They show you can think on your feet. They create a free flow. They create interaction. They help mesh your thinking with that of the client team.

LISTENING/OBSERVING

INTRODUCTION

Another important one-on-one selling skill vital in group selling is listening/observing. All of the one-on-one rules about being attentive—concentrating, looking at clients, taking notes at appropriate time—hold true for group selling. *The difference is that there is more to pay attention to and absorb.* It is harder to pick up cues or actually see what is going on because there is greater physical distance between you and the clients—and they usually outnumber you. Therefore, you must put your antennae up and use your team to help you pick up signals and interpret what is going on. The client who does not look at you, the client who grumbles, the client who scowls, the client who looks confused by a term or a point in your discussion, the client who is not paying attention, the client who is reading the proposal and not looking at you, and the client (or teammate, heaven forbid, but it happens) who falls asleep—all must be noticed and dealt with. You must be able to see and hear what's right and what's not.

"Read the room" so that you can determine how clients are reacting to you and what you are saying. Body language is there to read if you look for it. One sales manager who is legendary for making winning sales presentations tells his salespeople that at the end of the presentation, they should be so observant that they should be able to tell him "the color of the tie of the guy in the far corner."

By listening, observing, and interpreting clients' body language right from the start, you can gain insight into their reactions and adjust your presentation accordingly. It can even enable you to turn a situation around. One client in the group went so far as to immediately toss the proposal he had been handed away from him to the center of the table. The salesperson read this arrogant and disdainful gesture and made a point of spending the maximum amount of time, 30 minutes out of a 45-minute meeting, listening to the needs and perceptions of the group *before* positioning his ideas. By the end of the meeting the "gunslinger" hostility subsided; he walked out before the close but within one month the consultant had the business. After giving the consultant the go ahead the client said, "In your presentation you really turned us around. I think it was because you listened."

As you look at individuals in the group, notice whether or not your clients are looking at you. In most cultures, it is fairly safe to assume that when someone stops looking at you, he or she probably has stopped listening to you.

LOOK AND LISTEN

Observe what is going on. *Look at and listen to each client as he or she elaborates.* Information, even negative information or signs, can prove invaluable. Also show interest in what your teammates are saying. And of course, as clients speak, don't interrupt them. Let them repeat themselves. Listen for nuance differences, one different word. Don't tell clients you have heard it before. Listen to them and show interest in hearing more. Ask questions to get details. Listen to the specifics of what is on the clients' minds. Pause and use silences to make sure the client has completed his or her idea. Listen for key words and incorporate them into your response and listen between the lines to pick up feelings (listen for hesitations, voice that drops off, gulps—all signaling lack of confidence). Look for expressions of concern (shaking head "no"), puzzlement (furrowed brow), interest (two senior clients looking at one another), or satisfaction (nodding "yes"). By listening and observing you can get on your clients' wavelength and you can position your ideas accordingly. An investment banker describing a particular deal said that when he heard his client gulp over the telephone he knew "the guy wasn't in the deal."

One young salesperson, a junior on the sales team, made an excellent catch because of his powers of observation. He rescued his managing director when he noticed concerned glances between the CEO and Chief Operating Officer (COO) when the managing director mentioned the term "auction." The managing director, busy presenting, did not pick this up. The salesperson made a judgment call and interrupted the presentation. He said to the managing director, "Excuse me, I don't wish to be rude" (he prefaced his interruption in this way since he had not said one word up to this point), "but I think perhaps there is some confusion about the term 'auction.' " The managing director took the cue and straightened out what could have been a serious misunderstanding. The CEO called the managing director the next morning to say they would be working with them and added, "That was a good catch by your young man."

Unfortunately, another young attorney did not fare so well; after putting in two 24-hour days working on the proposal, he fell asleep during the presentation. The partner observing this passed a note to his team member who was sitting next to the young attorney. It read: "Bob is nodding off. Get him out and tell him to *stay* out." Of course, when it is a client who falls asleep, you cannot be quite as direct! In all situations you need to use judgment and tact. You should pick up early on the client whose eyes are closing or whose head is nodding; use his or her name and frequently look at and address comments to him or her. You might also ask questions. These tactics work most of the time. When clients are busy reading the proposal and not looking at you, you can regain their attention by being more directive, for example directing them to a particular page by saying, "I would like to cover the alternatives on page ____. Take a second to look at that and then let's discuss. . . .", or by using your eyes, voice, and body to get them to look up. Again, using a name or asking a question will help you regain eye contact.

POSITIONING YOUR PRODUCT/IDEA

Straight product selling is out today; positioning is in and indispensable. Unlike ten or even five years ago when there was greater differentiation among competitive products, competitive products today often look alike to clients, whether or not they *are* alike. This point bears repeating: clients often cannot tell one product from another. Even savvy clients such as the Hertz executive quoted in an April 1988 *Institutional Investor* are of the opinion that most products are the same. He said, "Most products do mostly the same thing. . . . [it is] the same product with six different names."

But really the problem is not so simple. Even though quality standards are improving, clients *can* tell differences among products, but often only *after* the selling phase. It is in the selling phase that they often find it difficult to distinguish the features and benefits of competing products. Very often, upon using products clients experience the differences in after-sales performance and their satisfaction. As the salesperson, you need to appreciate that they say your client may not easily see or believe these differences in the selling phase. They do not have your experience with the product.

In an environment of look-alike products, understanding and presenting your product's features and benefits is essential. Features are what your company puts into the product. They are the characteristics or attributes of the product or idea. Benefits are the value to the client. Benefits enable you to draw the conclusions for the client and drive the value to them home. Unfortunately, many salespeople talk features and, in doing so, sell themselves and their clients short. But even knowing your product inside out is not enough. Product knowledge is just the starting point. The key to selling today is in 1) *understanding the client* so you can relate your product to the client's needs, 2) *differentiating your product,* not only in its "inside" features and benefits but in the *outside* ones as well, such as expertise, post-sale performance, service, responsiveness, and quality. As one divisional president of a leading insurance company said, "We are the leaders in this field because we know our clients and our client's clients. If one of our clients says he likes blue my salespeople know if it's navy or azure!"

Certainly when your product has unique aspects (features and benefits), capitalize on them. But even if you have a unique idea, your clients need more than the inside features and benefits. They don't want generic information. They want ideas that are tailored to them, quality service, and relationships they can trust. The difference between product selling and need selling can be summed up in the difference between *presenting* (talking about the features and benefits of the product) and *positioning* (talking about the clients' objectives and how your idea or product matches up). But being able to "position" is predicated on knowing your client—very well!

TELLING YOUR STORY

Positioning is how you tell your story. The question is, do you want to tell your story from your point of view or your client's point of view? Of course, to position you have to understand what the client's point of view is. It's an old advertising maxim that the three most powerful words in selling are free, new, and *you.* Positioning allows you to bring the client "you" into the product. If you understand your clients, their strategies, their strengths, their constraints, you will be able to put the right idea on the table in the right way. Positioning will enable you to present your product so it incorporates what the client wants to achieve. If you put your generic product on the table, it will be up to the client to interpret how or if it fits. A generic product or idea is no match for a tailored, relevant product or idea, even if it fundamentally is the same idea. Someone who does feature/ benefit product selling is no match for a salesperson who can position with clients. As all salespeople know, a superior product can be rendered inferior by a poor presentation and an inferior product can look better thanks to a good one.

Positioning your products means that you discuss them in terms of what the client wants to achieve: client needs. Practically all salespeople when asked how they sell say they do *need selling*. But many in fact fall back on product selling. They may analyze needs but, when it comes to talking about their product or idea, many make sterile presentations that they could make to almost any client. In order to position (not just present) you must know your client and your client's business and industry as well as you know your product. Then you must mesh the client and product. Salespeople who really know how to position products are rare—one in thirty in my experience. What enables them to position the product is not their product knowledge (which is a given), but their client and industry knowledge. They know their client better than their competitors do, and it shows. Their products are simply the tools they use to satisfy client needs. They also know and believe in their own organizations and know how to leverage them.

The central idea this book aims to drive home is that your idea or product, no matter how good it is, will almost never sell itself in a competitive market. When you go into a competitive sales presentation today, you should assume that all your competitors—or at least one of them have good products and good people. Your objective should be to distinguish your product or idea. It is *how you* present that can help the client see the advantage of you and your product over others.

THE "HOPE CHEST"

I grew up at the end of the era of the door-to-door salesman and as a child I collected salesmen's samples (miniatures). My absolute favorite was a miniature hope chest, $10 \times 5 \times 4$. For those readers who may not be familiar with what a hope chest is, it is a trunk-like chest in which marriageable young women store items related to housekeeping in anticipation of their wedding day. I still own that miniature hope chest, and it has come to symbolize for me why product selling does not work.

All clients are the same in one way: They all have an objective they want to achieve. They do not want the product per se but they want what they feel the product will give them. The buyers of the hope chests were not buying the chest, but rather the dreams and hopes that they would put into them. In the same way, clients do not buy salespeople's products or ideas. They buy the achievement of their objectives, their hopes, and their dreams via the products. But as a salesperson, unless you take the time to understand and value what these are, you will find yourself selling "empty boxes"—empty products.

Positioning starts with knowing your client, and this of course means depth of information about the client's strategy, organization and operations and the clients' way of doing business. With this kind of information, you can incorporate the client's dreams, ideas, words, and situations into the product you are selling, and more importantly, you can help the client achieve the objectives he or she sets forth. For example, you might say, "Henry, your subsidiary in Cleveland. . . . we can give you the autonomy you need at the operations level. . . . and also. . . . for reporting. . . ." Price and product are important, but it is positioning that drives them home.

One top-performing investment banker brilliantly illustrated what it means to position when he explained to two entirely different clients why so many seniors had left the firm. To the first client, a traditional, family-held business, he discussed the tradition of his firm: He said that they thought of themselves as classes—class of '72, class of '76. He pointed out that of the X number of seniors who left *only two* went to competing firms. Of the remaining group he described three categories. The first category, the majority, were long time firm members who were tired of the ups and downs of the business and wanted alternative careers. The second category was the new hires to the firm who did not have a stake in the firm and had little motivation to stay. The third category were the individuals who just had not performed; yet, because things had been so good for such a long time they were allowed to stay for reasons of friendship and loyalty. When times got tough, he had to "let them go." He then discussed the new, excellent people he had hired, adding that for them, "We paid up." But the same facts were *re-positioned* when he was faced with the same objection from a tough, fast-paced real estate tycoon. Here the investment banker reversed the order and eliminated the "folksy" tone. The categories became the non-performers who were fired, the mercenaries who jumped ship, and those who had had enough to quit the business.

This banker has the highest standards of honesty and integrity with his clients. Yet, he knows the key to selling to a client resides in understanding that all clients are different and that you have to speak their language. By knowing his clients he can position his ideas in a way that make sense to them. He can speak their language and clients buy into what he has to say.

CHECKING

During a final presentation to a group of six clients, one client asked the salesperson, "How could your reporting system accommodate our need for a special. . . ." The salesman replied, "We can shut down the system . . . insert your criteria. . . ." Both the salesman and his manager felt relieved—even exuberant—that they were able to respond to the client's concerns. But to their surprise, they did not get the business. In turning the company down, the client said they were worried about the security of the system since it could be "shut down" so easily. Unfortunately, the salesman did not bother to *check* his solution to find out if his approach satisfied the client's concern. What the client interpreted wasn't what the salesman meant at all, but it was too late to explain. His competitor won the contract.

Checking—a vital skill at the agenda phase, during the body of your presentation, and at your close—is a specific way to question. It is the process of asking for client feedback each time you cover a point. In group selling, checking for client understanding is more important than it is in one-on-one selling and seems to be five to ten times more difficult (multiply by the size of your crowd!). If on a one-on-one sales call a salesperson forgets to ask for client feedback after covering a key point, the client is much more likely to simply interrupt him or her with the concern or show a sign of confusion with a puzzled look. But in a group environment, clients are less likely to interject their comments or ask questions, and you may be so absorbed in presenting that you may miss their telltale signs.

Unless you check, clients may listen quietly as you go out on a limb and start sawing! Remember, clients may not be staying quiet out of cruelty. They simply may not be that comfortable asking questions or may be conditioned to sit back and listen. The challenge is for you to change that behavior and get them involved.

Without a doubt, most people become quieter in a *new* group situation. When I was a teacher, it was my experience that about 90 percent of the students in my class did not voluntarily participate in classroom discussion until about the second week of class. Once they were comfortable with the new group and me, more than half of the class easily joined in discussions. The same holds true when selling to a group; but since you do not have the luxury of weeks to get clients comfortable, you must ask again and again, "Are there any questions?"

WHEN TO CHECK

Checking is one of the best ways for you to get client feedback and interaction and create a 70 percent:30 percent salesperson/ client mix. Good times to check are:

- *After you have presented your agenda.* Ask, "How does that meet your expectations?" This will set the stage for client particpation and give you the feedback you need to move forward or make modifications.
- *After you have talked for several minutes to see how you are doing.* Get feedback and create a *dialogue.* Say, *"On the points I've covered, what questions or concerns do you have?"* A swap team never bothered to check, and finally a CEO asked, "What is a swap?" three-quarters into their presentation. The team had to back up and begin with the basics. Although the other managers present knew these basics (the company Treasurer rolled his eyes when the CEO asked), the failure of the sales team to check early on set them back one month until they could reschedule a visit!
- *When people look bored, disinterested, puzzled, or, stop looking at you.* Say, *"We've covered . . . up to now.* Perhaps this is a good *time to get some reactions or questions."* You

can ask, *"Let's stop for a moment.* What questions or thoughts do you. . . ?" or "Let's pause here on the points I've covered. . . . What do you think about. . . ?" But remember, do not put anyone on the spot by singling him or her out. This is not the Army. Wait for volunteers! But if you know the client well and he looks puzzled, you might ask, *"Tom, you look like this may not be sitting right with you. What . . . ?"*

- *After you have answered a question or an objection,* ask, *"Does that answer your question"* or *"Joe, is this what you were driving at?".* This will show your sincere interest in satisfying the question and not just "showing off" your knowledge. And you will make sure you fully addressed the question.

- *Before you move from one topic to another or after you have presented a key idea.* After you have covered any part of the sales presentation framework (opening, agenda, need check, body, Q&A, summary, close), check if there are questions before you move on. Say, *"Before we move on to . . ., what questions. . . ?"*

- *Before you close.* Say, *"Before I close are there any other concerns or issues I could address while I am here?"* to surface remaining issues while *you* are there to address them.

Check to get closure so that you don't leave an issue or point floating in mid-air. This will help you nail down things. For example, a client said, "Other firms give us direct access to their New York traders." The presenter said, "We could do that," and left it at that moving on to his next point. He missed an opportunity to nail down a point and move toward an action step. He could have said, "We work very closely with our traders in New York. Tom Smith and our traders. . . . we would like to bring you in to meet them. Is coming into New York to meet Tom . . . something you would consider? After this meeting, let's look at when would be convenient for you."

Questions such as, *"What questions do you have on. . . .",* *"How does that sound?"*, *"Any questions?"*, *"Before I move on, would anyone. . . ?"* are especially valuable with clients who do not rush in to save you or who simply remain silent. *By helping force clients to say, "No, . . .", or "But. . . .", or "How. . . .", you give yourself a second chance.* Checking will help you gain closure on each issue before moving on to the next.

One salesperson presented his idea and moved on to pricing *without* asking if there were any questions or concerns about his product. The group sat quietly, looking disinterested. These clients were giving the salesperson more than enough rope to hang himself, which he in effect did by losing the business. In a one-on-one situation, a client probably would have interrupted with an objection, or the salesperson might have read the client's silent detachment.

Mayor Ed Koch of New York is famous for his checking: "How'm I doin'?", he asks. Checking says to clients that you care about them. While the risk of checking may seem high, it can save you if you are off track. Checking can provide you with the feedback you need to position, reposition, back-up, switch gears, or charge ahead.

Checking

AGENDA: • "Jim, does this meet your expectations?. . . . Is there anything I've left out?"

BODY: • "How does that sound?"
 • "Any questions before I move on?"

CLOSE: • "Before concluding, are there any other questions or concerns?"

• Remember: CHECKING SHOWS CONCERN, CONFIDENCE, AND CREATES CLIENT PARTICIPATION.

DEALING WITH CLIENT
OBJECTIONS

INTRODUCTION

Almost nothing causes more anxiety in a group selling situation as client objections. This is because the stakes are high and the credibility of the salesperson/sales team is at risk, as is the relationship with the client. Client objections in a group situation are challenging not only because you have to present information to resolve the objection, but also because in a group setting sensitivities are escalated and you need to put things in a way that does not offend or embarrass the clients. *How* you handle objections in a group is as important, if not more, than what you say, since clients generally are more sensitive in the presence of their peers. A comment that would be acceptable or open to discussion in a one-on-one situation can be extremely damaging in the "middle ground" of the peer group. The six critical skills are indeed critical here.

The CEO of an oil and gas company was attempting to buy controlling interest in another oil company. At a meeting with his board, the chairman of the target company used glowing terms to introduce the CEO. He praised the CEO's character and competence. Just as the CEO was about to thank the chairman for his kind introduction, a board member said, "He is a scoundrel. We shouldn't be talking to him for five minutes." In response to this insult, the CEO said in a soft, interested voice, "That's a strong statement." He then went on to clarify the objection by asking, "Do I know you? Which director are you?"

The director identified himself and then proceeded to discuss a negative experience he had with the CEO 10 years ago. As it happens, at that time the CEO was *counsel,* not a principal, in an oil deal in which the director had invested. In response the CEO described his role in the deal and revealed that he, too, was an investor. He then reviewed what had happened to oil prices across the board and asked the other directors where ten years ago they were predicting oil prices would go. He showed that the deal in question actually was better than most. He maintained his composure, got more information, and opened the discussion up to the group. He did not embarrass his attacker. As a result, at the end of this incident, all directors were apologetic and eager to move forward—which they did.

Unfortunately, many salespeople, when confronted with this kind of objection, don't fare as well. At best listen to the client without interrupting, present their rebuttal, and move on to the next point without checking to see if the client is satisfied. Just because the salesperson may be ready to proceed, the clients may not.

Let's look at resolving objections in a group selling environment to see the six critical skills (presence, rapport, questioning, listening, positioning, and checking) at work.

SIX CRITICAL SKILLS

When you face an objection, use all six critical skills:

1. *Maintain your presence.* Clients will observe and judge how you react to objections. It is important not to appear intimidated or defensive. Confidence and empathy will win out. Since the client is behaving aggressively, you should give him or her room by moving your body back *slightly* (an inch or so). But do not slouch, drop your head, or show signs of being crestfallen. Even if your nemeses pop up, for example, if your toughest competitor's name is mentioned as in, "We are talking to X.", or if a problem you were not aware of is raised, such as, "We were dissatisfied . . . in 1978. . . .", or "Someone from your company was here two weeks ago and he didn't know what he was talking about," or "We heard that already more than one month ago"—do not lose heart. Remain calm and confident. For example, in the situation in which a major competitor is mentioned say, "Very good. Then you have been looking at. . . . What. . . . and what I'd like you to do is compare. . . ." One top-performing-high tech salesperson who closes more big-ticket, complex sales than any of his colleagues or competitors attributes his success to his belief in himself. He says, "Other guys fold up their tents when X is mentioned, but I say 'Great, you've been looking. . . .', and then I proceed to find out what they like and dislike and then show our comparative advantages." Unfortunately, many salespeople become disheartened by tough objections and figuratively do fold up their tents. The problem is that clients can read this. You need to know what your "Achilles heel" is and be prepared to deal with it. How you hold up under fire counts, since the clients are judging what you are made of and how you will hold up down the road if they run into a problem. At the opposite extreme from being intimidated, equally problematic, is coming off arrogantly. While you may be standing up for yourself, if you do not do so with tact, more often than not you will be standing alone.

   2. *Listen to the complete objection.* Look at and listen as your client states the full objection. Do not interrupt the objecting client or show signs of impatience. Listen for broad or ambiguous words you will need to clarify such as, "The *risk* is too great." (What risk? Why is it too great?), or "Do you have an *office here?*" (What are they seeking to get through a local office?). Listen for neon words, the words that cause the client to light up, the ones that the client emphasizes with her voice or gesture. So that you can pick up on them, ask the client to clarify or incorporate them into your response. For example, a client may sit up or slap his hand on the table when he says, "We can't risk the *credibility of our name . . .* ".

   3. *Maintain rapport—show empathy for the client's position.* Do not offer a rebuttal the second the client stops talking. By waiting a second, you can show you are open to the client's concerns, and then by repeating the objection, you can begin the process of defusing and satisfying it. If a client says, "We just can't risk our reputation," or "We had an awful experience with you. . . . ", you could say, "Certainly I appreciate how well your name is regarded and how important your reputation is" or "I can understand how you feel," or, "Rick, I'm sorry to hear you had that experience. Certainly I can see how it could . . . and I appreciate your directness." By making a genuinely empathetic statement, you can help defuse the situation. Repeating the objection also allows you to *reframe* a negative comment, it helps you neutralize the situation, and it helps put you in the right frame of mind. But most importantly, it paves the way for you to ask the questions you will need to ask 99 percent of the time.

It is better to repeat the objection as closely as possible to the way the client states it to avoid misrepresentation. However, remember to avoid repeating extremely negative words, since that will further fuel the fire. For example, if a client says, "You are a bunch of crooks!" (hopefully this won't occur!) you might say, "That's a strong statement, and I am obviously concerned to hear you say it. . . . ", but you would not under most circumstances repeat the word "crooks."

Of course, you should never create a "show down" with a client or allow the situation to become adversarial on your part, *especially* in the presence of the group. But that doesn't mean you should skirt the objection. Unlike the CEO of the oil and gas company who was able to turn the objection around, one engineer went too far in his empathy statement and undermined his own position. Your empathy comment should communicate that you care; but, it probably should not express your agreement with the client. When the engineer's client said, "You're going to lose this one; you are too expensive," instead of expressing empathy with the client's need to get the best pricing and then finding out more about why the client thought he was too expensive, he joined right in and gave further credence to the charge by saying, *"I know many of our clients are saying that."* This engineer was his own worst enemy. His response showed a lack of confidence in his pricing. After expressing empathy, the engineer should have found out what he was being compared to. A question such as, "I appreciate the feedback and I want you to know that in working out your numbers I sharpened my pencil. I know cost is an important consideration for you. So that we can compare things side by side, what's included in their offer?", would have given him the information he needed to compare cost and value of both offers.

Another salesperson was highly effective in maintaining rapport when under attack. The risk manager said, "Why should we renew with you? You stuck it to us two years ago when the market was hard. Those increases were criminal." The salesperson, newly assigned to this relationship, had done his homework. He replied, "I know the rates were raised X percent in 1986. Judging from your comment, Tom, I think we must have done a poor job positioning it with all of you. As you know, it was a hard market and we were glad we could be there for you when other firms were not writing this kind of insurance at all. Obviously we failed to discuss how low, considering. . . , rates were very low prior to that and we needed the adjustment. Before '86 how would you describe the rates we were charging? . . . We value the relationship. . . ." By putting the blame on his firm for not presenting the rationale properly, by having done his homework, by reminding the client gently that *all* other firms pulled out of the market, and by asking the client how he would describe what were by anyone's estimation very low rates prior to the hike, the salesperson was able to resolve the objection and renew the contract.

4. *Ask a question to get below the surface of the objection.* As with the objections mentioned above, most objections are broad, too broad to answer. When a client offers resistance, you should ask yourself, "Do I know enough about what's really bothering this client to address it?" It takes discipline not to jump in with an answer, especially since the natural tendency for most salespeople is to talk. If you do not know enough (and unless you are clairvoyant, you probably don't), then you need to ask questions. Too many salespeople spray-paint their answers from their generic answer can, but never get beyond the surface of the objection. By asking for more information you can gain insight into what you are up against. The CEO of the oil and gas company asked, "Do I know you?" to uncover how the director came to the conclusion he was disreputable. He then asked the other board members, "Where did you think your product oil prices would go?" to get their support for his position. Asking questions brings the client into the problem solving process. But most importantly, it will also enable you to provide an answer that addresses what is on the client's mind. By showing empathy first you can lay the groundwork for your question.

5. *Position your response.* Once you have listened to the client, unless you need to ask an additional question, you will be able to position your response to address underlying objections rather than give a spray paint generic answer. The CEO of the oil and gas company was able to clarify that he was not a principal in the deal and was able to discuss the merits of the deal relative to the environment they were operating in. (Please see "Positioning," Page 111.)

6. *Check.* As a way to make sure that you have satisfied the client's concern and to determine if the point needs further discussion, check for agreement and understanding before moving on to the next point. Say, "How does that address. . . ?" (Please see "Checking," Page 116.)

Of course, satisfying an objection is not "one stop shopping." You may have to repeat the process of maintaining your presence, listening, relating, questioning, positioning, checking, etc. several times to work through one difficult objection.

One salesperson was able to preserve a major relationship by using this six-part process. One of his largest clients had recently reorganized its training department. Their full-time training manager had resigned, and instead of replacing him, they created a rotating training-manager position to be filled on a quarterly basis by a line salesperson. A salesperson was assigned and he was eager to make his mark. During the first few weeks of his tenure, several training companies, other than the one he was using, called on him to solicit business. Based on his discussion with one of the companies, he concluded that he was overpaying for his entry-level sales training. He called in the "incumbent" training company to meet with him and his staff. Five minutes into the meeting he said to the training consultant, "From all I've heard from my predecessor and from this group, you've done a good job for us. But, frankly, for our entry-level recruits, I just can't justify the premium price we are paying you. Perhaps the $650.00 a person can be justified for our senior people, but definitely not for entry level. Competitors I've spoken to who have been in to see me several times (stated with a tone of self-importance), and who are eager to work with us, are quoting a much lower price—half to be exact. I feel we should let them do the training."

The salesperson, faced with the threat of losing this account, knew he had to do something fast. Should he discuss the merits of providing new people with the best training? Should he lower his price? Fortunately, he decided he needed much more information before he could respond.

Many salespeople in hearing this objection would do one of several things: 1) disagree with the client and present the benefits of providing entry-level recruits with premium training, 2) lower the price, or 3) agree with the client that they are premium priced and accept the client's decision because of pricing! But none of these tactics—not even lowering price—would really satisfy this client. First of all, he might conclude that they had been taken advantage of and, second, price was not the only issue.

What would you do? He did not become defensive; he did not argue with the client about the need for premium vs. non-premium training for entry level. He did not even try to justify price with value—yet. He *kept his head, even though this significant, large client* was at risk. He had listened carefully. Between the lines he heard a wounded ego—Why hadn't he been in to see the new training manager? His competitors had been there. He drew on all six critical skills. Calmly, interestedly, he said, "Thank you for saying we've done a good job. We very much value our relationship with you and all the feedback from our trainer is also very positive. I appreciate your having this candid discussion with me. (Presence, empathy.) While I don't know every competitor, from my knowledge of our major competitors we are equal to or very slightly *below* their pricing, so I am concerned to hear you feel we are premium-priced. I can understand how you would feel if this were so. I would appreciate it if you could tell me who you have been talking with so that we can better understand what we are being compared to? Often in training, factors (such as the number of days for the seminar, minimum number of participants, and trainer and material fees can substantially effect the pricing. Can you tell me about the program you were referring to?" (Ask Question to Narrow Down Objection.)

The client declined to reveal the name of the competitor, but he did say that he didn't get specifics about the number of days of the training, or whether or not trainer fees or materials were included.

The salesperson then positioned his reply, "Sometimes pricing is quoted differently based on the number of days of the training seminar and the number of participants per program or in total," he continued, "whether or not the trainer fee is included, whether materials are included, whether or not you are using our trainer or your internal trainer? To help me understand . . . since from my knowledge of the market, we are not higher priced than our major competitors, may I ask that once you get the details if we can then compare. . . ?"

By the end of the discussion/problem solving, without anyone saying so it became clear the client was most likely comparing apples with oranges: In fact the competitor had proposed a two-day seminar, while his was three days; the competitor had an additional fee for the trainer, while his company did not. During the first meeting when the salesperson raised these points of comparison, he did not press for an answer from the client to help the client save face, especially with his staff present. Once the price issue was addressed, the salesperson broached the subject of "premium-*quality*" training for "MBA entries" (new people who hold MBA's) given their demanding and vocal nature.

Even once the training problems were settled, the salesperson knew he had a bridge to mend. He had been negligent in not meeting the new training manager. To compound this, he didn't even know the previous manager had been replaced! However, he did know his new client had three needs: 1) a business need—not to overpay, 2) an ego need—to make a change, after calling the meeting with his staff and the consultant, and 3) an emotional need—to feel he was getting the attention an account of his size warranted. To address the ego and emotional needs, the salesperson set up a follow-up lunch and suggested changing the configuration of the training days, *not the price.*

He used the six critical skills to resolve the objection:

- **Presence**—He did not become defensive or intimidated in manner or tone.
- **Rapport**—"Thank you for saying we've done a good job. . . . "

- **Questioning**—"Can you tell me who you have been talking to so that. . . ?"
- **Listening/Incorporating**—"To tie back to what you said. . . . "
- **Positioning**—"Sometimes pricing is quoted differently. . . . "
- **Checking**—"Can we get back together once you get the details?. . . . If you feel two days seem more appropriate at the entry stage, we can modify the agenda. . . . I can send a revised two-day agenda to you. How does that sound? We could then add on the third day later to reinforce. . . . What do you think?"

The salesperson was able to resolve the client objection by engaging in joint problem-solving with the client without creating a show down. He used the six critical skills to get beyond the tip of the iceberg to understand and satisfy the objection. His relationship with the new client decision-maker continued to develop, and over the next two months he gave him four referrals to other groups within the organization.

PREPARATION— PREPARING FOR THE SALES PRESENTATION

INTRODUCTION

Preparation is the first and most important element in winning more business. A highly successful managing director at an investment bank attributes his success to his detailed preparation. He tells his team members that they literally should know "what they (the client) had for breakfast" to underscore the importance he places on being prepared.

Being prepared takes homework. It means being thoroughly *grounded* in your proposal, knowing more than, not just what is on each page. Preparation includes knowing:

- CLIENT NEEDS—What does the client need?
- CLIENT DECISION-MAKING UNIT—By whom and how will the decision be made? What are the politics/sensitivities?
- YOUR OBJECTIVE—What do you want to achieve?
- YOUR STRATEGY—How will you approach the situation—with whom, where, when, and what?
- YOUR IDEA/PRODUCT—What product/service will you present to satisfy that need? What are the alternatives to

your idea? What competitors are selling? How will you position your idea/product?

- YOUR TEAM—With whom and how will you present? How will you take advantage of your seniors, specialists, colleagues, and juniors?
- THE SETTING—Where and when will the presentation take place?
- TIMING—What is your lead time to prepare? How much time do you have to present?
- PACKAGING—What materials/proposals/visuals will you need?

Being prepared means you know your client, your organization's resources (people and products), your product/idea as it relates to the client, alternatives to your idea, market and industry factors, and who your competitors are. The precious minutes you are given for your sales presentation are like the seconds in a T.V. commercial. The 30-second claymatic commercial for California raisins ("I heard it through the grapevine") took 12 weeks at $3,000 per second to produce. The amount of time and money it takes to prepare may seem disproportionate to the actual amount of time on camera, but the proliferation of such high-cost, prime-time extravaganzas indicates that the investment is well worth it. A sales presentation is in a sense *your commercial* and every minute is critical (in a commercial every *second* is critical). Often the culmination of months of time, marketing, networking, and nurturing, the sales presentation gives you time to *score your points with the client.* But unless you are *prepared,* you'll waste that precious time.

CLIENT NEEDS

Because today's clients demand *relevant, tailored ideas,* preparation truly pays off. Nothing can take the place of homework to help you understand your client's needs and objectives so that you can present the right ideas in the right way. Homework with the client face-to-face and/or by telephone, homework outside the client organization, and homework within your organization will provide you with the information you need. Once you understand the client's strategy, goals, needs, and decision-making process, you will be able to develop and position ideas that make sense for the client. One investment advisor, the "dark horse" competing against two top-tier firms won the account. His was the *only proposal* that would provide the client with the *liquidity* he needed to grow his troubled division. He was able to create the right structure because he made it a point to ask one additional question after in-depth discussions with his clients: "What would your ideal solution include?"

Clients themselves are usually the best source of information about what they need. Clients know their issues, concerns, and political sensitivities, although it is easy to forget this. When approached correctly, clients are usually more than willing to provide you with information if they believe there will be a payback. How easily available information can be simply for the asking was demonstrated by an engineer. Just as he was ending a telephone conversation, he asked his prospect, a high-level contact at a Fortune 100 company, the key criteria his company were *really* looking for. The client succinctly rattled off three points. When the engineer complimented him on the precision of his answer, the client mentioned that following a weekend team-building and strategy session, they had written a paper describing their strategy and organizational structure. The salesperson asked if he might find out more about their conclusions to help him prepare for his presentation. The question did not offend the client, who actually volunteered to fax a copy of the paper to him. When the engineer was awarded the deal, the client said, "We felt you all understood where we are headed better than anyone else."

Questioning in one-on-one situations before your group presentation can give you a tremendous edge. In the past, before the sales spotlight became directly focused on the client, such in-depth questioning was not as crucial. Salespeople knew to ask open-ended questions, but selling was more talking than listening. Today the emphasis has shifted. To adjust to this change, you need more information. By asking *indepth* questions you will be able to tailor your presentations.

Expand your questions to include:

- Decision-making questions—Organizational questions to find out who is who and how decisions are made.
- Relationship questions—"How am I doing?" and "How are my competitors doing?" questions to find out where things stand.
- Operational questions—Technical questions of how, how many, where, and why.
- Problem questions—Questions to identify what obstacles the client is facing.
- Situation questions—Today and yesterday questions to find out what the client is doing.
- Strategy questions—Big-picture, tomorrow questions to find out where the client is and where the client is going.
- Interpersonal questions—Questions to get to know/understand your client.
- Need questions—Questions to find out what is not working and what needs to be fixed.

I use the acronym "drops^2-in" to help prepare my list of questions. Nothing in my preparation is more helpful to make business "drop-in." "Earn" would indeed be a better acronym, but the letters don't work!

Also, keep in mind that all clients have two need levels: business needs, related to organizational and product needs, and nonbusiness needs, related to their personal goals/emotional requirements. Your objective should be to learn something about both, for all clients in the decision-making unit, especially for clients in the power base. To get at their personal needs, find out: What are their business orientations? What are their backgrounds? What stake in the deal does each have? Why? Who has an ax to grind? What role will each play? What is the attitude/preference/point of view of each player? What does each player know about the product being presented? What are their points of view? What are their areas of expertise? What are their personal interests/politics/sensitivities? What are their buying criteria? How do they like to be sold to? What are their preferences for sales presentations: proposals, slides, technical details, the big picture? Being unaware of personal sensitivities cost a money-center bank a big deal. The small Florida bank it was trying to buy opted to merge with the money center's competitor. The reason: the winning bank provided for the small town bank president to keep his office and the local prestige that went with it.

Homework on nonbusiness and business needs can help save a precarious situation. One salesperson learned that a strong influencer in the client group was lobbying against his idea for a leasing program. The client perceived the new approach as a threat to everything he had accomplished over the past five years because the new system would dismantle what he had put in place. He feared being discredited with his seniors. The salesperson learned about this resistance through his contact, then arranged to meet with his would-be antagonist one-on-one. He discovered that this client was the originator of the previous system, which indeed was ground breaking in its time. At his group presentation, the salesperson began by praising the innovation of their present system, giving credit to the client for breaking new ground and making the approach he was proposing possible. He showed the progression sincerely without being obsequious. By the end of the presentation, the influencer supported the idea. He said, "Here on my note pad I had written all the objections that I had coming into this meeting. But each one has been crossed out by me. Bill has logically and clearly presented his case and I support it."

CLIENT DECISION-MAKING UNIT

One salesperson recounts what he calls "the ambush." He and his three team members were sitting in the conference room where they were to present as their five clients marched in. His colleague whispered to him, "See the woman with the red hair? I broke off a two-year relationship with her three months ago." The salesperson attributes their being able to save this situation to a combination of his colleague's split-second decision to walk out of the room and not participate in the presentation, the integrity of the woman, and the quality of their presentation. That was the last time that team failed to identify all the players on the client's side before meeting with them! Situations such as this underscore how important it is to know the make-up of your client group. Of course, even when you do your homework, there can be surprises. When this happens, be positive, flexible, and welcoming, but avoid accepting new players at face value. Take the time to shake hands and meet or greet everyone individually. Get to know your contact to find out tactfully who the newcomers are, what their roles are, and why they are there. In doing so one presenter identified a competitor in his midst! He was able to mention his concern to his client, who in turn asked the competitor to step out of the room. Unexpected players is just one more reason to arrive early so that you have time to make the introduction and do some intelligence-gathering.

But knowing who pulls the strings in the client group isn't always easy. In one of the most challenging group sells I have ever experienced, I had to present to 25 decision-makers, three times. After being one of five competitors, one of four, then one of two, we were finally their choice. Why? We knew that with a decision-making group of 25, a few key individuals would be far more influential than others. Through homework we were able to identify the three individuals who formed the power base and would swing the buy decision. We also discovered a fourth key influencer during the presentation not included in our original list. He was the president of one of their smaller subsidiaries. While he did not say very much, he commanded the attention and respect of the group. He sat in the center of the group at the central table and invited other players to express their opinions. We made it a point to find out the needs and orientation of the key players and we gave them a discrete amount of special attention, such as more eye contact or looking to them for feedback first. In addition to this, we built our presentation progressively, learning from each presentation what the company did and did *not* need; then, we further tailored our proposal each time. Before each subsequent presentation we tactfully asked them what they liked and didn't like in our and our competitors' presentations. By contrast, our competitors *repeated* their *canned* presentation. Their loss was our gain.

A space planner learned how important it is to know who is who and to be courteous to everyone. She had worked long and hard to win the opportunity to present a space plan to the treasurer of a major telecommunications company. When she arrived, she was surprised to find that she and her manager would be meeting with five clients, not four, as planned. The new player began making suggestions that the space planner found outrageous: the department should have pink walls, the treasurer should have a sofa near his desk, etc. When the planner tried to present her proposal, the mystery client said, "You don't understand. John [referring to the treasurer] likes to be close to his people." The space planner responded firmly, "No, *you* do not understand. . . .", and continued her presentation, cutting the woman off from further remarks. Later, the space planner learned that the mystery participant was the treasurer's wife. Had she know this, she might have used better judgment and more skill in responding to this individual (or for that matter, any member of the client group) with, "Thank you for pointing that out. Having an environment which people can communicate openly is important. May I ask how you envision. . . ?"

Another salesperson who did not do his homework on who was who wasted too much time trying to resolve an objection raised by one of the clients. To his dismay, he learned minutes *after* the presentation that this individual, with whom he had spent about eight minutes of his 45-minute presentation by trying to resolve his concern, had resigned one week before and would be leaving shortly. A simple question such as, "Can you run through who X & Y are?" to his contact in the one hour meeting they had before the presentation could have saved him at least half the time.

One of our consultants was hired away from us by one of our valued clients. She was immediately solicited by our key competitor. He was selling sales training; yet he never uncovered in eight sales calls over a year and one-half, that she had worked for us, his number-one competitor, nor did he ever bother to find out her opinion of us, her present training vendor. He didn't ask questions. He didn't practice what he preached. He didn't get any business from her.

All of these examples point to the need to know who you are selling to. *The information is there for the asking, but few salespeople ask.* Your contact in the company, or better yet, your "coach" (the individual in the client organization rooting for you from the chairman to administrative assistant) can be an excellent resource, giving you the general overall political picture, individual information, and invaluable insights. For example, one specialist, thanks to help from his bank's relationship banker, succeeded in getting the mandate for a Eurobond based on the guidance and insight provided by the company's cash manager, who for years had a close relationship with the relationship banker. If you are wondering if among your clients you have developed coaches, you can give yourself the litmus test. Ask yourself which clients have your home telephone number and you theirs.

Better than learning secondhand about the individuals who make up the client's decision-making unit is learning directly from each individual what his or her needs and interests are. You can do this by meeting with each client *one-on-one prior to* your sales presentation. This personal contact beforehand can help reduce client fears and antagonism, if any exist. Not only can this provide you with information, but it will help you establish rapport, minimize surprises, prevent obstacles from arising, and position your idea.

If you have the opportunity to meet clients personally, one-on-one, it is foolhardy not to do so. While groundwork takes time, it is well worth the effort if you want the deal. If you cannot meet each player one-on-one prior to the sales presentation, you may be able to speak with each person by telephone. Sometimes, of course, neither face-to-face nor telephone contact is possible and you must get information indirectly from your contacts in and/or outside the company. The problem with this point of view is the needs expressed by the operating officer from his or her own perspective may be different from those described by the chief executive officer. It is in these situations that the need check is most critical.

A warning about one kind of decision-maker who has killed more deals than almost anyone else: the new player. This individual often is mentioned casually: "Oh, we have a new. . . ." Look upon the entry of the new player as the tip of what can be a very cold iceberg.

Don't be fooled into underrating the significance of the new client as one salesperson did. He had one last hurdle: the *ideal* final presentation—one with no competitors. The day before the presentation his liaison in the company called him to say, "Oh, my boss would like to see you the hour before your presentation." He agreed to a 10:00 A.M. meeting and inquired if his boss would be joining them for the 11:00 meeting with the line managers. He was told "probably not." This sale was "sewn-up", so why bother to do homework on the new person? He thought incorrectly. Not surprisingly, the project the salesperson was to close on was completely and artfully sabotaged by the new player who felt that the project encroached on her area. Before the group meeting she got to two key influencers who said as if on cue at 11:00, "We don't need outsiders. . . . Sally can do it." The group decided to have *her* conduct a study! The salesperson was put on permanent hold. The lesson learned is that there is no such thing as an unimportant last-minute player!

Your own organization also is an important resource to help you learn about client decision-makers. There is a saying that "Everybody knows somebody." This seems to be true. To learn as much as possible about individuals, first you must find out who knows whom. These resources may be in or outside your own organization. Then, of course, you tactfully need to tap the sources and even more tactfully put the information to use.

The information is more often than not available for the asking. Time and again, salespeople who ask get the information they need, and those who don't ask, lose out.

Once you have information on the players, you can develop a strategy and prepare for either a solo or team sale. So before you venture into making your presentation, find out:

- Who is in the decision-making group?
- Who is included in the power-base unit?
- Who are the key influencers?
- To whom does the primary economic decision-maker listen?
- How will the decision be made?
- When?
- *Who* (names/titles) will be present at the presentation?
- Who is behind the scenes?
- What are their functions?

Once you have identified key people, ask yourself these questions about *each one:*

- What is his/her role?
- Where does he/she fit in?
- What did he/she think of the project?
- How does it relate to his/her area?
- What does he/she want?
- What stake does he/she have in this?

DEVELOPING AN IDEA AND OBJECTIVE

In the May, 1986 issue of *Institutional Investor,* 24 "Choosy Treasurers" revealed how they selected their investment banks. The overriding reasons they gave were *relevancy of ideas* and *execution capabilities.* All clients want products that make sense for them and products that deliver what they promise. Clients ask themselves, "Will this help me meet my objectives?", and then, "Can they do it?"

While clients say they crave original ideas, saying, "Bring me a *new* idea," they may really be saying, "Help us solve our problems." They want something that makes sense *now,* new or otherwise. Certainly, an original idea has great value, especially in breaking into a new relationship. But clients are satisfied with ideas—old or new—that help them achieve their goals.

Developing a relevant idea is step one. It requires creativity and analysis. Without a good idea, there is nothing worthwhile to present. But once you have a relevant idea or product, step two is to *position* it so that the client can appreciate it. Good ideas/ products simply won't sell themselves in today's market. Mrs. Field of Mrs. Field's Chocolate Chip Cookies recently said on national television that her product is so good it "sells itself." But when pressed about how she actually got customers to buy it, she said that when she first opened her store, *she failed,* so she decided to give the merchandise away and close the store. The non-paying customers got hooked and came back to *buy* more cookies. Mrs. Field's cookies, in fact, did not sell themselves. What did sell Mrs. Field's was an inadvertent free-then-pay strategy. The company continues to use this try-then-buy approach by still offering free samples of every cookie type. Cookies are baked in clear view of the customers, literally positioned to get customers to try then buy.

Giving free samples of ideas is more difficult than letting a customer see and sample cookies. Nevertheless, your task is to position your ideas in ways that allow the clients to see them, believe in them, and want them.

One computer company hosting a client seminar did not position its product to match the customers' interests. They presented their *generic product* to a group of 30 lawyers and certified public accountants with disappointing results. Few of the participants stayed to ask questions after the presentation and none returned telephone calls afterwards. Because the presentation failed miserably, the presenters concluded that their most serious error (out of a *long* list of mistakes) was their failure to tailor the new product (a micro-computer) to the lawyers' and CPAs' businesses. The salesperson acknowledged, "It didn't occur to me until *after* the seminar that we should have talked *their business,* not micros. We still haven't gotten one referral from them yet. . . ."

In both your written proposal and your oral sales presentation, you need to spell out your idea or product so that it reads "client." Clients want to see *their* own names in lights, not yours. (Please see "Positioning," Page 111.)

Like a one-on-one sales call, your group selling presentations should have a measurable *objective* and a time frame for achieving it. This objective is your point of destination: where you want to be at the end of the presentation. It is what you want to walk out with. It can be helpful to think about your objective as one side of a coin with the client's objectives as the other side. It takes both sides to make the deal work. Presenting the client's side of the coin (what the client wants) is the best path to getting your objective.

As you develop your objective, also think about your target objectives as well as your presentation objective. For example, your target objective may be to get the deal, but your presentation objective may be to end with a statement of your next step. Too often presenters are ineffective in their closing because they have not articulated their objective to themselves and, hence, don't articulate it to their clients. (Please see "The Close," Page 58.)

SETTING A STRATEGY

YOUR TEAM

Team selling has become a way of life today. Because of the increasing complexity of business, the need for specialists, and the need to match up levels with players on the client's team, you will often find yourself involved in team selling. Also, because clients have been "burned" by disappointing experiences, many now demand that the people who do the selling are the ones who will be working on the project.

There are advantages to team selling: bringing in expertise, balancing the numbers, matching client levels and types, providing a learning ground for juniors, and increasing resources since two heads are better than one. Additionally, team selling can shift some of the pressure off you and demonstrate to your client the depth of your organization.

But there are risks, too, in team selling. During the sales presentation, everyone on the team (junior associates, colleagues, specialists, and seniors) will be under scrutiny. Almost nothing can be more damaging to your sale than letting your team show lack of unity. Clients will not only be evaluating you, they will also judge *each* team member. One consultant lost a small but important project with a Fortune 1000 company because he included a brand-new person on his team. Including this new person was his first mistake, but *not* positioning the rookie as such was his second, fatal one. When one of the clients directed a question to him which he failed to answer, the team's credibility was destroyed. Keep in mind that the greater the number of individuals you include on your team, the higher the margin for error. There is a parallel with *IBM,* which has recently decreased the number of parts between generations of products. Their strategy, to produce products with fewer parts (from 2,300 parts for a Selectric typewriter to 190 parts), has increased the product's reliability by a factor of 10.

So, if you are selling with a team, in order to reap the benefits and avoid the perils, demonstrate teamwork. And this takes work. Since nearly everything gets done informally in most organizations, you need to build an internal network to ensure the support you need when you need it. By establishing a positive, personal (not memo-based) network across divisional lines throughout your organization and in your own department *before* you need your colleagues, you will be positioned to mobilize resources to achieve and get the support you need.

Team Leader

First and foremost, there should be *one* team leader ultimately responsible for "calling the shots." One salesperson describing how his firm won an important contract said the real challenge came from *inside* his organization, not *outside.* Initially, the product specialist refused to participate if the sales generalist— a buffon, is his opinion— participated. The team leader finally said, "I've worked hard for this and I'm calling the shots. I know what we need and we need both of you. I'll talk with him about . . ., but I need your support. I've been there in the past for you!" This unified team won the deal. In one company, the two salespeople making a call on a company's management team decided at the end of the call to write separate thank-you letters because they could not decide who the lead was. Needless to say, this reflected poorly on them and their organization. It boils down to knowing and respecting "Who's on first?"

Assembling the Best Team

One pressing problem organizations face is deciding who should and should not participate on the team. Too often political and territorial considerations interfere with assembling the best team. Teams with too many players or the wrong players are at a disadvantage. How many should be on your team can be determined primarily by *who is needed and who is best able to close the deal*. The criteria for organizing your team should be:

• First—the internal resources and expertise you will need to win the deal. What specialists/experts/support will you need? Who can help ensure you will get this deal? For example, for a deal you may decide you need three people: the first, a senior, to set the stage; the second, a product specialist, to present the idea and pricing; and the third, the account generalist, who knows the client and can build a bridge to him or her and help establish credibility for the team.

• Second—the number, the level, the areas of expertise of the clients who will be present at the presentation.What levels will be present in the client group? If the presentation is to the CEO, CFO, treasurer, and attorney, then your team probably needs a senior, a financial and legal person. As one client aptly put it "If a client is spending hundreds of thousands of dollars, he wants to shake hands with the president."

Once you know who will participate on the client's team, you will be able to match up your team with clients. For example, in presenting to a Japanese client group you should match the senior level in your organization exactly to the senior level in the client group. You can also look at other factors such as "fit." For example if the client is "very laid back," it would be foolish to walk in with three "Green Beret" types. If the client team is all over 50, it would probably help to include someone of similar age in your group.

• Third—your judgment and internal considerations. Who is best qualified to make the sale (Who can best bring the ball across the line)? Who should present what? Who should attend as a perk? For example, a junior person may have worked around the clock doing research for the presentation, preparing the proposal, or developing the materials. If other factors are in line, i.e., if you do not far outnumber the client team, you can include this junior person, not only because you may need to get more information on the research, but also as a reward and learning experience for him or her.

In putting together your sales team you need to be sensitive not only to who is on your team, but also to how many players are involved. In one company, team sell was so glutted that the salespeople themselves jokingly referred to it as a "_____ swarm"! with the name of their company preceding the word swarm.

You don't want to overwhelm your clients by sheer numbers or make them feel you are ganging up on them. A group of three clients is apt to feel overwhelmed if seven of you descend, unless, of course each of you is essential to the deal. In addition to this, if you include unnecessary people on your team, you could inadvertently communicate to the client you are insecure. When sales generalists are asked why they want so many specialists to "tag" along to a sales presentation, they often say they want to be prepared for whatever comes up. They would be more effective if they qualified the opportunity before the meeting and placed some of their colleagues "on call," rather than engage in overkill. Clients don't like an unnecessary entourage either, and they often comment, "So-and-so was here, but he didn't say a word!" Recognizing this, however, it is the complexity of the deal and the resources you will need that is the final determination, not the number of clients. As a rule of thumb, there is only *one* leader, and each team member should have a role, even if it is only a small part. Everyone should know his or her part in the presentation and time allotment. Each participant should know what is expected: seniors on the team may be there to wield influence and juniors to run the numbers. *One* team member, almost never more, can be allowed to attend as a learning experience.

Do not allow internal pressures to weaken the team you ultimately put together. One successful manager admonishes, "Hurt their feelings!" (referring to colleagues you should *not* include). While this kind of approach eventually would be detrimental to you internally because "what goes around comes around," (a lot sooner than you think) you do need to find ways to convince all involved parties what is best for a particular presentation. One tactic you could use involves asking would-be team members or their managers why each proposed member should be included and what his or her role would be. While you need to be sensitive to political considerations in your own institution, your primary consideration has to be organizing a winning team.

Once you know who is on the client's team, you will be able to assess who you need to match up. For example, one salesperson's homework revealed the client's primary concern was its German subsidiary and that two people from the subsidiary would be on the client's team. The salesperson included on his team a colleague who had worked for a major German corporation. This team member helped set the presentation strategy and proved invaluable in both establishing rapport and relating to the German clients.

One organization had to go outside itself to form a winning team. It proposed financing for a mining venture for a major multinational and presented its plan to the client group. In his "morning after," telephone call the presenter learned that the multinational company still felt it should get bids. The clients candidly said they were concerned that his firm did not have mining expertise. The presenter asked for a chance to revise his proposal and return for a second presentation, a joint venture with an outside geologist he brought with him to the presentation. They won the contract.

Regardless of each team player's role, all team members must be alert, interested, and supportive throughout the presentation. One sales team won a piece of business with the provisio that a certain person on the sales team *not* work on the account. The client said, "You and Richard were so interested, involved, but she seemed bored." Even team members who do not have an active role, have an important role. Simply, by virtue of being there, they are a part of the sales equation, and clients count them in their overall evaluation of you. Also, since it is difficult for the person presenting to see or hear everything going on, the other team members can and should jump in to help in an appropriate way. For example, the senior presenter made an error in discussing a cost per item. His associate simply passed him a note which read, "$25 or $18?". The senior apologized and retracted the figure. Had the associate not been sitting close enough to slip the note, he could have addressed his senior, "Excuse me, Mike, but could you check that price?" He then could have read in the eyes or observed in the next step of the senior whether or not he had to spell out $18.

Team Preparation

Coordinating your team on the plane, in the cab, or in the elevator simply is not good enough today. As a team you need to agree on a strategy, concur on your objective, and define functions and roles. Everyone—generalists, specialists, seniors, associates, operations, etc.—needs to know what is going on and what is expected of him or her.

Once you organize who will lead and who will be on the team, involve them early to help you formulate your proposal.

Team members' roles need to be coordinated, especially the roles of specialists so that their talent can be leveraged. The generalists often know the client and the specialists often know the product. Only by dove-tailing the two can you position the product or idea properly. Whatever your strategy, once it is set, all of your team members should be aware and committed to it. In orchestrating your team, work out:

- Who will lead?
- Who will make introductions?
- Who will open?
- Who will present technical information?
- Who will handle the broad issues or political questions?
- Who will discuss pricing?
- Who will close?
- Who will take *notes*? (This is *not* the lead presenter's responsibility.)
- How and when will you signal or correct one another?
- Where will team members sit/stand?
- Who will write the follow-up letter?
- What is everyone's role?

If the meeting is to be held at *your* site, plan:

- Who will schedule the conference room?
- Who will make sure all players know what, where, and when?
- For out-of-town clients who want to come to your home office—what entertainment—dinner, theatre, sports events—should be planned? With whom? When?

It is my view that selling to client decision-making teams is a *razor's edge business:* the salesperson or the sales team who makes the best presentation will have a distinct advantage. Most companies are selling quality and clients cannot easily differentiate features and benefits from one product to another. They can differentiate people. So don't let internal political considerations or egos get in the way of putting forth the best team before the client. Practice with team members and, if all team players have heavy schedules, then at the very least set a time *before* the presentation when all team members are present to prepare/practice.

Team Guidelines

Some guidelines for organizing and preparing your team are:

- *Plan together; practice and work at it!*
- *Discuss the client group that will be present.*
  Analyze needs and strategy (business and non-business needs).
  Identify client players and their roles.
  Review interpersonal information, personal traits, background, familiarity with your institution, and product and/or situation.
- *Set your sales objectives and your desired outcome.*
- *Determine and resolve major presentation problems.*
  Design and agree on roles in the presentation, roles in the preparation, deadlines individual team members must meet, information to be researched, materials to be prepared, amount of time to present, travel arrangements to be made.
- *Determine your team members' roles.*
  Pare down unnecessary players.
  Decide who will present what.
  Plan who will open and how.
  Plan who will close and how.
  Agree to support each other 100 percent during the sales presentation.

- *Assign tasks.*
  Identify your team coordinator or team leader.
  Prepare an outline of what you will cover, questions that need to be asked/answered.
  Develop your proposal.
  Prepare visuals, communicate with your graphics department.
- *Set deadlines.*
- *Communicate progress and status periodically.*
  Get one another's home telephone numbers.
- *Network in your organization.*
  Identify and tap all the resources you can use.
- *Rehearse.*
  Evaluate your proposal/idea.
  Evaluate delivery skills.
  Identify areas for improvement.
  Prepare for objections and questions and role play the situation.
  Check for brevity and clarity.
  Check your timing.
  Determine areas for improvement and *make them!*
  During your sales presentation, remember that you are a team and *support, listen to, look at, show interest in,* and *help each other* as well as the clients.

TIME/TIMING

As a part of your preparation, think about how much time you will have to present. Determine how much information you can reasonably communicate in the allotted time. Most salespeople sooner or later overestimate what they can include. This mistake of "overstuffing the goose" can cost them the deal. For example, a successful market-research salesperson, accustomed to having one hour to 90 minutes to present to four to eight clients, was asked to make a 20-minute presentation to a task force of 15 department heads. The client had invited a total of seven firms on the same day as a preliminary screening.

The salesperson used his usual "full-blown" approach. He was just warming up when he learned his time was up. The client liaison interrupted him by saying, "You have just about three minutes. Do you want to summarize?" He had barely opened! He had not presented the essence of his approach. He had no time for Q&A.

The result of this poor presentation was no sale. He actually became one of three finalists (which gave him insight into the quality of the other competitors!), but in the end the deal went to a competitor. Instead of bringing finalists back as initially planned, the client made the final decision based on the 20-minute presentation! This very large piece of business was lost. The client told the salesperson, "You were Number Two, but the group really didn't understand what it was you would do. . . ."

The lesson here for all presenters is to know how much time you have and to plan accordingly by setting an objective that can be accomplished in the time frame. It is not possible to fit all of a one-hour presentation into 15 or 20 minutes. When you are alloted such an abbreviated time, you will often be in a "beauty contest" from which only a few finalists will emerge. You need to headline each part of the sales presentation framework to give the overview. If the salesperson had taken a *headline* approach, (Opening, Agenda, Needs, Body, Summary, Q&A, and Close), he would have used his 20 minutes this way:

> Opening—two minutes to introduce himself and his company;
>
> Agenda— one-half minute (or skip the agenda phase, just two or three bullets at most);
>
> Needs—four minutes to state his objective and have clients identify key areas they want addressed;
>
> Body—eight minutes;
>
> Q&A—four to five minutes;
>
> Close—one minute.

Preparation Time

How much time you have to prepare is a crucial consideration. Ideally, you would have sufficient lead time so that excessive time crunches don't occur. But this is often not the case. Many deals have been won by *sheer determination* on the part of the presenting team willing to work through the night or over weekends to capitalize on a window of opportunity. Because of fierce competition or when you face time pressures, you need to put in the hours to mobilize a winning team.

A salesperson boasts of a real-estate deal he sold, but the real source of his pride stems from *how* he sold it. At 8:00 P.M., one week after he presented an idea to a New York-based company, as he was flying to New York from Los Angeles, he learned via the air telephone that his client had scheduled a full presentation for 8:00 A.M. Monday morning. All members of the salesperson's team had also been away during the week. Time was of the essence because the window on their idea could close at any time. The salesperson spent Saturday morning getting home telephone numbers of the specialists he needed and he, the specialists, and his manager spent Saturday and Sunday preparing for the presentation. They met at 6:30 A.M. Monday to run through their parts, and by 8:00 that morning they were presenting to the client. The elation after they closed the deal was as much for orchestrating this winning team as for the size and uniqueness of the deal with a prestigious client.

Choosing a Time Slot

Which time slot is best? The answer to this in part depends on schedules and availability. But most salespeople don't appreciate how important timing can be, and they fail to ask the few simple questions like, "May I ask how many presentations there will be? Who will be presenting? What are the time slots?", that would enable them to position themselves in the "best" slot. *Most smart salespeople want to be last, especially when the sale presentations by competitors span a few days.* The companies that present on Monday may be a blur in the minds of the clients by Thursday.

Being able to schedule your sales presentation as the last in the series of competitors gives you the advantage of working with a more educated group. It allows you to put the ideas your competitors have presented into perspective and gives you the benefit of having the last word. The only time not to take the last slot is if it is likely that key clients won't be there—for example, if three presentations are called for the morning, with the last one scheduled after lunch.

Also, if you are given a choice to present at 11:00 A.M. and then have lunch with the client at noon, or have lunch at noon and present at 1:00 P.M., the latter is probably your best bet. There is an old saying in sales: "After you ask for the order, put on your hat." This will also give you "warm-up" time and an opportunity to gather more information and insights.

Rely on your judgment to determine the best time to present. Regardless of when you are presenting, arrive in sufficient time to set up your room and build rapport with clients. Time is an asset. Use it. Capitalize on what you deem to be the best time slot. Arrive early so you can set up your room, meet people, test equipment or hardware, and rearrange seating if necessary.

PRACTICE

Practice does not make perfect, but it does make professional. Nothing gets more lip service than the importance of practice. Most salespeople and sales teams simply don't practice. They say they simply don't have the time. But when you consider the time and expense in finding the opportunity, in pre-presentation selling, in preparing materials, in developing and mobilizing a team, and then in making the presentation, it becomes clear that sales presentations are an expensive proposition. Your sales presentations will make a lasting impression. More often than not, getting the business will hinge on how you do then and there. Even if you don't win the business, the impression you make *will count for the next time* in the minds of the clients. With so much at stake, the payoff for an hour or so run-through more than offsets the cost in time. Not only will it help you become more familiar and comfortable with your proposal, but it will also allow you to time your delivery, try out different approaches, and get feedback from your manager, peers, or team members. When all else fails, set a pre-presentation time to rehearse on/near the presentation site. But do not practice up to the minute before schedule to present unless there is absolutely no choice, to keep your presentation fresh.

One of the Big Eight accounting firms understood the value of *thorough* preparation. Although it is not common for a major company to change accounting firms, this firm found itself in the desirable position of taking a significant piece of business from a competitor who had slipped up. The dissatisfied client, an insurance company, had opened its door to bids. This Big Eight firm attributes its winning a multimillion dollar piece of business to its preparation. They used their one-month lead time to plan their strategy, organize their team, develop their proposal, do their homework, and PRACTICE. On three occasions they went through the presentation with all six of their team members, including their chairman and a senior partner. In place of the 12 clients they used cardboard dummies (no reflection on the clients). They worked out every conceivable detail and anticipated every possible objection and question. When they finally got to the clients, they were organized, knowledgeable, and confident. They felt they were the best for the job and convinced the client of it. They attribute this coup to their practice sessions.

It is extremely helpful to practice *aloud* prior to your presentation. This is infinitely more effective than a silent mental review, since it will let you hear and feel how the presentation will come across. Practice your opening, but don't memorize your opening sentence unless you are an accomplished actor, because it will not be as effective as spontaneous but prepared comments. Know what you want to say and say it. Commitment and confidence in your voice is better than perfectly recited sentences that sound flat.

Of course, wherever possible, participate in as many group selling situations as possible since participation will give you the opportunity to practice and refine your second set of selling skills. No amount of practice will let you anticipate exactly what the scenario will be, but it will help you be as ready as possible. In fact, you should aim for at least 25 percent of your prepared presentation being improvisational, based on what happens on the spot and the give-and-take with the clients. Presenters who win deals are prepared, but they also can think on their feet. Indeed, it is through preparation the improvisational part works.

If you are not prepared, you *should* be nervous! Knowing your subject and your audience, while not necessarily antidotes for nervousness, will allow your other anti-nervous strategies to work. (See "Nervousness," Page 80)

THE SETTING

The environment in which you present is more than a mere back-drop. It is a "player" who can add to or detract from how you come across. Most of the time you will be required to present at the client's site. It is your responsibility to make the most of the environment you find and not become its victim. Certainly by having the client at your site, you have the advantage of controlling the environment and minimizing distractions. Al-though this is not always possible or desirable, there are ways to maximize any environment you are given.

The best way to take advantage of the environment is to find out what the physical setup is *before* you make your presentation, so you can capitalize on advantages and minimize constraints. If you cannot visit the site, you should at least inquire about it. But even this can lead to problems. A salesperson called her client to ask when it would be convenient for her to have her flip charts delivered. The client who was in the oil industry, assured her it was not necessary to bring her own flip charts since their new conference room was equipped with two of them. When the sales-woman arrived, she discovered that the design firm certainly didn't have her in mind when they constructed the facility. The flip charts were suspended from the molding on the ceiling, per-fectly accessible for someone 6 feet, but totally out of her 5'2" reach!

Almost all environments have pluses and minuses. Your goal should be to take *control* of the environment by being as self-reliant as possible. For example, if your presentation is dependent on an overhead, bring your own small, portable one. Carry your own extension cord. One firm, after waiting two months to get an appointment with the chairman of a major company, learned when they arrived that the chairman's new carpet covered every single outlet. They were unable to present their slide presentation because neither they nor anyone else in the executive suite had an extension cord.

Unless you pay attention to details and know what to look for, the setting can work against you. One computer company learned this when it made its presentation to 25 potential clients from the business community. They scheduled it to follow a breakfast, seating all 25 clients around three tables. Although the presentation was based on a product and depended on the concept of "a terminal at every desk," they provided only one terminal. Furthermore, although they did project the reports onto a large screen, they did not have anyone to guide the clients in understanding it. Nor did they provide hard copies of the reports to illustrate their points. The presentation was a monologue with no interaction.

Opposite is the case of the local sports medicine center that did everything right for its opening. It began with an autograph signing by members of the city's professional football team and T-shirt giveaways—a sure way to get people there on time. Following this was a presentation on the center's facility and services. Then they closed with a sign-up for the facility tied to a ticket drawing for an upcoming game—a great strategy to keep the audience there for the close.

Seating Arrangements

Regardless of where you are presenting, you need to consider the seating arrangement. You must consider where you (and your team) will be *relative to the clients*. A rule of thumb is not to be far away from the key decision-maker; get as close as possible to the key decision-maker.

By arriving early, you can often create an environment apt to work best for you. For example, you can move furniture around. If there will be a total of eight participants at your sales presentation (three on your team, five on client's team) and there are twelve chairs, if possible move four chairs against a wall so that there are *exactly* eight seats around the table. This way you will not end up with empty seats (black holes) between people. If you fail to do this almost invariably you will find yourself surrounded by empty chairs, not clients.

Of course, you need to use judgment about how much furniture moving you can do. You cannot move chairs in someone's office (sometimes you can ask). You should also look around or ask your contact to make sure you do not take an inappropriate seat, such as the chair the chairman always takes. In choosing where you will be, do as much as possible, for example, putting your teammate directly across from you to avoid a "lock-horns" position in which you are sitting/standing directly opposite the key decision-maker. "Lock-horns" setups with clients create adversarial situations. There is no harm in asking the client, "Where will you (or X, the key decision-maker) be sitting?", and then choose your seat accordingly, hopefully at a right angle to him or her.

When possible you should also avoid the "us" against "them" arrangement with the two "sides" lined up against each other on either side of the table. Simply ask, *"May we scatter around?"* Your goal would be to get an OK to mix in with the clients. In some situations, you, of course, will just arrive and take seats because everyone is already seated. Think about ideal seating and then do your best to approximate it based on what is happening. Remember the old Scottish saying, "Wherever McTavish sits is the head of the table!" You can be the leader from any chair with the right delivery and "presence" and sometimes not taking the "lead seat" can be effective in disarming the client group.

Before you are to present, *look* at the room. If you are number six, following five other presentations, the room may be scattered with junk. If the clients are taking a break, without being conspicuous, clear away miscellaneous materials (junk, trash, empty coffee cups, filled ashtrays). If the client has a carousel or other equipment set up you will not need, move it; roll up the screen and so on. If you need a side table for your materials or slides, ask for one.

Be sure to *remove any signs of competitors*. A presenter went through his complete presentation without noticing that his competitor's bigger-than-life logo appeared in the front of the room all the while—perhaps a deliberate strategy.

Before you begin, walk around the room and look at the spot where you will be sitting or standing from where the clients will be sitting to make sure that you will be visible to everyone. One presenter making an after dinner speech was told by a senior vice president that a candelabra blocked most of the left side of the room from seeing him!

Standing and Sitting

You can maintain presence whether you stand or sit. Depending on your strategy, the client's culture, the number of people, and the setting, you can decide whether to stand or sit. Whether you are sitting or standing, your presence can say that you are leading the meeting. *Getting near the group* is important because it creates an environment conducive to interaction and give-and-take.

Standing is usually more appropriate when the occasion is more formal, when you are using visual aids or equipment, or when you are addressing larger groups. When you stand, eliminate barriers between you and the group whenever possible (table or podium) since they physically and psychologically separate you from the group.

Sitting, my preference, is appropriate in less structured settings or when you are addressing a smaller group of three or ten clients. Sitting with the group can create a more intimate environment. It can also make it easier to create interaction, since all players are on an equal level. When you are seated, let your posture tell the group you are leading the presentation. Whether you are talking or listening, sit "at attention" and do not slouch. *Inch up* in your chair to emphasize important points and project confidence. *If you are seated in a swivel chair, do not swing back and forth.* When possible don't sit in a swivel chair. You can also combine sitting and standing. For example, begin by standing, sit as you begin to go through the analysis in your book/proposal, and then stand when using flip charts, slides, etc. Variety will help you communicate that you are confident, in control, and will help you project presence.

In summary, take control of the environment. Don't be a victim. Check:

- What will the room be like?
- Where will you sit/stand in relation to your clients?
- Are the seats arranged in the best way? Can you avoid empty seats between clients and management and you/ your team?
- What can you do to improve the environment? Can you clean any junk away before beginning?
- Where will you stand/sit, show slides, etc.? Can everyone see you and your team?
- Did you check your equipment? Do you have everything you need—extension cords, etc.?

GROUP SELLING PLANNER

To help you prepare for your team presentation, you can use the following Client Analysis/Team-Coordination Worksheet and Group Selling Planner. This form is not a form for form's sake; rather, it is a discipline. Since group selling is more complex, developing a written plan will help you think through all of the pieces and organize the players.

GROUP SELLING PLANNER CLIENT ANALYSIS

Your Objective_____

Benefit of Objective to Client (Purpose):_____

Client Decision-Making Unit	Business/ Product Needs	Non-Product Need	Feature and Benefit Related to Client Needs	Objections/Issues
Economic Decision-Maker(s): Name(s)—Indicate if they will be present (P) or not present (NP) at your Sales Presentation: • • •				
Influencers (Advisors, Technical Specialist, User, Coach, Other): Names/Function: • • •				

YOUR TEAM COORDINATION

Your Team Structure—Names	Role	Element of Proposal or Responsibility for Team Member	Time Allotted
• • •			

Logistics: Place_____ Time_____ Materials_____ Equipment_____ Refreshments_____

Business Entertainment:_____

(Please note who will be responsible for team coordination, developing the proposal, making introductions, providing expertise, showing senior-level commitment. . . .)

(Complete and copy for each team member.)

158

SALES PRESENTATION FRAMEWORK

Client Name:_____   Product:_____

Client Contact:_____   Sales Team: _____ Lead: _____ Team: _____

Date of Presentation:_____   Time:___ to___   Place:_____

Opening (Client Need/*What's in it for the client?*)

Opening:

Introductions:
  You:
  Your Team:
  Your Organization:

Agenda (Overview of key points you will cover in your presentation)

Overview: "Today I will cover. . . ."

Checking: "Does that meet your expectations?"

Client's Needs (Participation)

Anticipated Needs:

Need Check:

Body (Idea/Proposal/Recommendation)

Key Features (Inside & Outside):	Key Benefits to Client:
Anticipated Objections:	Responses:
Key Topics to Cover:	

Summary

Final Summary Points (what you want the client to remember):

Q&A

Close (What do you want the clients to do?)

PRESENTATION SETTING

Materials	
Visual Aids:	Place:
Proposal/Handouts:	Time:
Equipment:	Equipment:
Materials:	

Self-evaluation for Practice Session	
Strengths:	Areas for Improvement:

PACKAGING— DEVELOPING THE PRESENTATION PACKAGE

INTRODUCTION

While your written proposal can not sell for you, it can cost you points if it is not up to par. What to include, what to leave out, and how to package ideas are factors that can help move a sale forward or stop it.

A major architectural firm attributes its losing a 50-million-dollar opportunity to renovate a historic train station to what proved to be an inappropriate presentation package. The 25-minute television-quality video production they decided to use was all wrong for their client. Although the team of 12 professionals who would have worked on the project were present during the video presentation, feedback from the client after the presentation revealed they did not get the deal because the clients found the approach too slick and impersonal. The clients said they could not ask questions or respond to what was going on. Since good video is extremely difficult to do, it is possible that the video just missed the mark. But it is more likely the medium itself was the mistake because every word of the presentation was "on record," giving the sales team no opportunity to massage and position their ideas other than the formal brief Q&A at the end. Unfortunately, many salespeople use their written proposals in much the same way. First, let's look at how to package your ideas, and then how to use your proposal.

As you develop your proposal, you should give painstaking attention to every detail. As Francis Bacon, the Renaissance philosopher, noted, "Reading maketh a full man, conference a ready man, and writing an exact man." Think exactingly about each draft and seek out criticism from seniors, specialists, and other team members. Study examples of successful proposals your organization has on file. Access all available information and resources to make your proposals as effective as possible. Whatever you include, regardless of how little or how much, must be well thought out, accurate, and tailored. Since the sales presentation/proposal stage is often the make it or break it stage, clients are *not* tolerant of errors. So get it right!

To help you format the proposal, find out how the decision-makers like to see information and what their culture is. You may find the CEO likes bullet points, not prose, or that he or she likes extensive detail or prefers slides. One presenter learned too late, after making his slide presentation color-coded, that the CFO was color-blind. You can save time and money by finding out client preferences or idiosyncrasies. Consider the political as well as the business situation, the business and nonbusiness needs such as ego, in order to exclude embarrassing information.

ORGANIZING YOUR PROPOSAL

The organization and flow of your proposal should make sense from both a presentation and a sales viewpoint. One salesperson began his proposal with a statement of his objectives as Tab 1 and followed that with pricing as Tab 2. His pricing section was out of place from a presentational and selling point of view. While the client may ask for price first, you, as the salesperson, need to position and control the pricing discussion so you can link price to *value*. The salesperson would have been more successful had he brought up pricing *after* he presented and positioned his idea.

While there are no absolutes as to how to structure a proposal, there are guidelines you can follow in developing your sequence:

• *Include an introductory section.* This should be made upon a cover/title page, table of contents, and executive summary. The cover page should include the names (and logos when possible) of both your *client* and *your organization.* A table of contents can quickly give an overview of all the categories in the proposal; include page numbers or tab numbers. When you need to make last minute proposal changes—for example, to include market-sensitive information, you can forego page numbers, *but* be sure to use numbered or labeled tabs. Tabbed materials are easy to work with, provided there are only two or three pages per tab. Even when you have page numbers, tabs can be an asset. The information included in the table of contents often will match your agenda. You can use the table of contents as an agenda for a less formal presentation or you can develop a separate agenda page. Your executive summary will provide an overview of your *idea* and how it works for the client. Make sure it communicates the essence of what you want the executives to know. You can make a part of your proposal or create a more extensive executive summary. For example, one leading firm always prepares a five-to-seven-page executive summary book used during the presentation backed up by a more detailed book. Appreciating that it is unlikely that seniors will read 15 or so pages, they develop strong, short executive summaries that seniors are likely to read.

• *Start out your proposal by stating the client's objective.* State the client's objectives, needs and strategy to indicate to the clients that you understand what they want to accomplish. Get this information from the client and use his or her words! My colleague who was required to work with another firm on a project said that she was amazed that this firm reworked their proposal three times and still did not get it right. She said, "They kept coming back with their proposal, never using the client's words and I certainly wasn't going to teach them!"

• *State your objective.* Position what your organization proposes to do in light of the client's needs, making sure it incorporates client needs.

• *Describe your idea.* Outline relevant features and benefits of your idea or product related to what the client wants to achieve. Position your idea so that your product/features and benefits match the client's *needs.*

• *Present your financial analysis* (cost justification). Tell how the idea benefits the client financially. For example, you may need to cover accounting or legal issues. Consolidate information here to several pages, then put back-up detail into an *appendix.* Include graphs, etc., as needed and interpret what the idea means to the client's bottom line. If appropriate, describe *risk/opportunity.* Describe potential benefits vs. risks if appropriate, or when you wish to position yourself as an advisor if there are risk and opportunity nuances in alternatives.

• *Reinforce your institution's "value added"* (differentiation). Tell the advantages of working with *your organization* and you. For example, an investment bank might include tables showing its standings and its key players, or a manufacturing firm will provide a record of its quality performance.

- *Present your pricing structure.* Present price and tie it to value.
- *Outline your summary points.* Wrap up with approximately three key summary points you want the client to remember.
- *Include an appendix if necessary.* Consider using a *second book* to keep your primary proposal usable, client-friendly, and approachable. Use the appendix as needed throughout your sales presentation. The appendix can contain detailed information, back-up information, your track record, references, your team, your timetable tied into the client's timetable, etc.

Certainly, the structure of your proposal needs to be based on your knowledge of your client, the type of product you are selling, the purpose of your proposal, and the culture of your organization. These general categories can, however, serve as guidelines. Most importantly, the proposal should reflect the client and not be a dry, technical, product-driven document. A proposal can range from a one-page sheet to an extensive document. You can also consider developing two proposals: a brief "executive proposal" and an in-depth back-up proposal.

Please note, however, that if a client, for example, a governmental agency, sends you its own format, *you should follow it.* One agency sent 10 corporations just such a bureaucratic request listing 20 questions to be addressed in the presentation. The companies that followed the format were considered, while those who did not were disqualified. If you do not follow the formula dictated, or if you fail to address issues the client has identified, you may lose the opportunity to compete. Sometimes government agency formats are deadly, and while you must follow them, you can overlay additional information and subcategories such as a table of contents, executive summary, introduction, etc. Note, however, that these additions should not interfere with the numbering sequence prescribed in the agency's blueprint.

One warning about written proposals. Be sure that yours is warranted. Clients sometimes ask for proposals as a smoke screen when what they really mean is they are not interested. Also salespeople often get out of an uncomfortable situation by saying, "Let me send you a proposal" when they should be qualifying and identifying needs.

One way to tell if a proposal is indeed appropriate and not just generating work and paper is to ask yourself if you have the depth of information you need to tailor it. Clients and salespeople serious about a proposal are willing to take the time to identify the information they need. When clients request you send a proposal say, "Yes . . . what do you want to achieve. . . . what would you like included, so that I can. . . ." Clients who resist giving you information may be less than genuine in their request, and salespeople who don't ask for information may be spinning their wheels.

PACKAGING

One salesperson missed out on a multimillion dollar deal for what could be described as a 25-dollar reason. A comparison of his proposal to the winning institution's package revealed some startling differences. The competitor's handsome proposal, packaged in a gray folder, had been prepared on desktop publishing software, and was tailored to incorporate the client's objectives throughout. The salesperson's proposal on the other hand had been typed, copied on a poor quality copier using flimsy paper, and stapled. It contained a diagram *without* arrows featuring two boxes which read "Bank" and "MNC" (for "Multinational Company")—not even using the client's name! More incredibly than this, the salesperson used the generic term "Bank" instead of the name of his own bank! The quality of the package was inferior by any standards. When his manager reviewed this proposal after the fact, he was understandably angry. His anger was further fueled when he asked the salesperson to explain the diagram and he drew the arrows in the wrong direction.

Of course, attractive packaging cannot compensate for an irrelevant idea, inaccurate information, or poor group selling skills. But when relevance, accuracy, and skills are in place, packaging can be the finishing touch. It says something about how you work and how you will execute. It also remains with your client and their management or staff after your presentation. If you are required to submit a proposal in advance (which is not the ideal situation since it limits your flexibility and ability to personalize), good packaging can also help get you in the door.

Clients will grade you not only on your idea and how you present it, but also on the appearance and structure of your proposal. Because mediocre packaging can tarnish the brightest idea, look critically at your proposal to make sure that it speaks well for you. If it is not organized from the client's point of view and not packaged in a professional way (e.g., paper quality, print quality, folder, etc.), it will do *more harm than good*. While the packaging does not have to be slick, it has to be professional and "client-friendly."

Proposal packaging means even more when it is the proposal, not you, that the ultimate decision-maker sees. Sometimes, regardless of the reason, the client, him or herself may be the one to present to his board or seniors *without* you. On other occasions, you will be required to send your proposal in advance of your presentation. When these situations arise, you must labor even more diligently over every word, figure, and detail of formatting and packaging to create that edge. Also, check with your client whether any part of the proposal (pricing, etc.) should be eliminated for general review. The appearance of *each and every page* will help or hinder getting your message across.

Before we look at general packaging guidelines, let us consider one of the technological miracles of our age—the fax machine. Combining the speed of the telephone with the tangibility of overnight mail, telecopiers have edged out both technologies in the past few years. Salespeople fax away when they need to transmit signatures, receipts, and documents, or to cancel appointments with clients they cannot reach by phone. Clients do the same. But while such fast action can save business, it can also blow it.

Although fax technology is new, it has already generated some classic war stories. The most horrific one I have heard yet came from the president of a major paper manufacturing company. His company's million-dollar-a-year contract with a major client had expired, (while paper costs had skyrocketed). Instead of arranging a meeting, the busy salesperson (business was great!) faxed a new proposal to the company's purchasing manager. The client faxed back! He would pay 75 percent of the increase, but 100 percent was out of the question. The salesman discussed the client's counter proposal with his president and faxed again: The 100 percent increase was firm.

The fax communications finally ceased when the client called this salesman to tell him he had put the job out for bids and that his firm was not even being considered. The president intervened to save the account, virtually pleading to get the business back. He assumed total responsibility for the error, and then refreshed the purchasing officer's memory of the exceptional service he had received for the past 12 years. In the end, the president agreed to a 75 percent increase.

The moral of the story is simple: when it comes to selling or negotiating, under most circumstances, face it, don't fax it. The fax machine, like the telephone, as wonderful as it is, depersonalizes contact and limits flexibility. Had the salesman and the president handled this differently, with follow-up by fax, it is likely they would have gotten 80 percent, 90 percent, or even 100 percent of the increase.

PROPOSAL CHECKLIST

Here is a checklist for assessing the appearance of your proposal:

- *Cover/folder for Proposal.*
  Is it attractive, professional?
  Is there a standard folder that you can use?
  Is it tailored to your client, with the client's name/logo *and* yours on it?

- *Format.*
  Are the pages numbered?
  Are tabs called for?
  Is there one subject per section/tab?
  All sections placed in the order in which they will most likely be used?

- *Page Format.*
  Did you highlight key ideas on each page?
  Is the format consistent? Are all titles bold/caps? Are they

all underlined? Is there consistency in terminology?
Is the layout attractive and does it involve/invite the reader?
Is each part tailored to the client's situation, and does this show up in headings?
Are *client benefits* included and highlighted with headings?
Did you use only short paragraphs when appropriate with headings, bullet format, and visuals/graphs? (Avoid page-after-page blocks of prose.)
Did you use color?
Is the quality of the print up to standards/readable?
Is the paper top-grade quality? Do you have special paper/letterhead for your proposal? (Do not just use what happens to be in the copy machine.)
Does your firm's name/logo appear on all proposal pages? While the focus should be on the client, the client should be reminded whose proposal it is.

- *Binding.*
  Is the package bound in a professional manner with spiral ring or attractive binding, not merely stapled?

- *Diagrams/Graph/Charts.*
  Does each diagram have a *heading* telling what it is?
  Is each diagram, flow chart, etc. personalized whenever possible?
  Are arrows in place and pointing in the right direction?
  Does the diagram show the benefits or points you are trying to make? Put a caption under each diagram.
  Do the diagrams relate to the proposal?

- *Organization of Information.*
  Should you use tabs?
  Are tab headings in the most effective order?
  Is detailed back-up technical information handled in an addendum or separate book?
  Did you identify all analysis so that you get credit and inhibit competitors from helping themselves to the infor-

mation? For example, for financial analysis, unless you say, "Prepared by _____(your institution)" at the bottom of appropriate pages, your clients may think you got it from them!

- *Leave-Behinds.*
  If your client has the proposals but you use overheads, slides, etc., that are not covered in the proposal, should you use leave-behinds—for example, copies of slides not included in the proposal?

- *Content.*
  Don't forget content. Is it relevant, accurate, and tailored to the client?

USING YOUR PROPOSAL

Developing your proposal is the beginning. Since clients are not as familiar with your materials as you are, your role is to guide them through it. *Many salespeople rely too heavily on their proposals and hide behind them.* Instead of reading the group, they read their proposals. *Your proposal can show the depth of your preparation.* And even though many clients will not read every word, they will to a certain extent give you credit, simply for volume, for having done the work. But that is as far as it goes. It is up to you to use your judgment in how extensively or minimally you use your proposal. Use it to *amplify* what you have to say, not replace it.

Let's look at the most effective ways to use your proposal.

PRESENTATION PHASE	USE OF PROPOSAL
Opening, Agenda Check and Needs Check	Normally you would not have distributed your proposal until these three elements have been completed. But you can distribute your proposal before the agenda check if you want clients to have a copy of the agenda as you go over the agenda.
Body	You can use your proposal throughout the body to: • discuss your client's situation, objectives, and needs; • present your idea/product and how it addresses the client's needs;

PRESENTATION PHASE	USE OF PROPOSAL
Body (*continued*)	• document your recommendations and information; • reinforce your value-added, and • present pricing
Summary, Q&A, and Close	You may or may not refer to your proposal during your summary or Q&A. While there should be a summary page in your proposal, you should not read it to the clients. It is much more important to have eye-to-eye contact as you begin to wrap up. Do not use your proposal as you close.

The following guidelines will help you *use* your proposal effectively:

• *Don't read to clients.* As you present your proposal, do not read it unless you are reading figures or new technical information. Talk about it; look at someone.

• *Don't necessarily go front-to-back.* Use your proposal flexibly as you need it. For example, with a client group very familiar with the product, you may quickly go through several tabs and focus on others. Use your proposal as a tool to help you communicate with your client. Use it to help you present your ideas, offer back up information, provide details, and underscore points.

• *Present your proposal.* Whenever possible, present your proposal in person. Your proposal can't sell as well as you can. If you are not there, you won't be able to position your ideas based on feedback. When a client requests that you send your proposal in advance of a presentation—or worse yet, in place of your presentation—set a follow-up appointment whenever possible at that time. When you are asked to send a proposal in advance, find out who will get copies. This enables you to take all of the clients' perspective into account and allows you to send the appropriate number of copies, saving the client the trouble of making copies as well as safeguarding the quality of the copies the decision-makers and influencers get.

When you must send your proposal in advance, include a cover letter thanking the client, a list of your capabilities, an outline of the proposal's major sections, and what your follow-up step will be ("I would like to thank you for your consideration of our proposal. . . . Based on our discussion, I am sending you. . . . Thank you again. I will call you on. . . ."). Of course, even when you have sent copies in advance, bring extra copies to your presentation for forgetful clients. Although there are strong offsets to the risks of sending the proposal in advance, there is at least one advantage: you often can get feedback to use to *modify* the proposal *before* your actual presentation, saving valuable time in the agenda check. So be sure to call and ask for feedback and make appropriate changes.

• *Don't present a proposal that will shock your client.* Don't go into a lion's den. Once you develop your ideas, bounce them off your client contact in advance to get feedback so that you can go in with a proposal that will result in good business, not a good-bye.

• *Be familiar with your proposal.* Avoid having to hunt through your proposal to find information, especially if you were not the one who developed your proposal. Prepare thoroughly. You should know where things are and where they come from. Annotate your copy with numbers and comments so that you don't waste time searching or groping for information: "Please wait. I know it's here somewhere. . . ."

• *Distribute your proposal when you are about to use it.* This is usually *after* you have opened or as you go over the agenda. One of the most common mistakes salespeople make relative to proposals is that they place them at each client's seat before they begin. When this happens, clients more likely than not will be flipping through the proposal and miss the opening. Do not give out copies of your proposal until you are ready to use it or you will be in competition with your own materials. Unless there are too many people (more than 30) *and* it would be very difficult to distribute materials during the presentation, *do not distribute* materials until you are ready to use them. A small but significant gesture, especially with a smaller group, is to hand each client his or her copy of the proposal, saying each client's name as you go around. This small touch can help you personalize, build rapport, and create the intimacy possible in one-on-one. Be sure your team members also have copies.

• *Develop an executive summary.* Since it is unlikely that a top decision-maker such as the CEO will read 15 or so pages, it is a good idea to include an executive summary to outline the key points of your proposal.

• *Don't bring a tome.* So that your proposal is not overwhelming to clients consider using two proposals: your presentation proposal as a brief outline of your categories and an in-depth back-up/addendum.

Guiding Clients through the Proposal.

Clients need to be directed as they work through your proposal with you. Here is what you can do to ensure your materials are a help, not a hindrance.

• *Make sure all clients have copies.* Make sure you have sufficient (extra) copies of your proposal. When you do distribute materials, look around to check to see that each client and each of your team members has a copy. Check, "Does everyone have a copy?"

• *Guide clients through pages. Number pages or tab small sections so that clients can easily find them.* Having to say, "Turn three pages from the back" or "The page that starts with the word 'tax' " will detract from the professionalism of your presentation. As you discuss a particular page or handout, always tell the group the *page number* and heading. Say, "On page ____, you will see at the top. . . ." Look and wait a second for clients to find the page to which you are referring. Say, "Please turn to page ____ to find _____", and then see if clients are following along. If last-minute changes make it impossible for you to number pages, you can use tabs (providing each tabbed section has only a few pages in it). Highlight important information with different typeface, color, or boxes.

• *Check as you go.* Check before moving on to other sections. Say, "What questions do you have up to this point?"

• *Read the room.* How the clients use or don't use your proposal can provide insight into whether they are with you, are ahead of or behind you. Reading the room can also be invaluable with neutral or positive clients since it will give you cues as to your pace and when to refocus. For example, if you see that a client is on Page 15 when you are on Page 2, you can provide discreet nudging such as, "So as you can see on Page 2. . . " to help the client refocus. When one of your clients is rushing ahead of you, you can say, "So on Page 2 you can see. . . ." So that you don't embarrass anyone, it is better to do this as a general comment rather than direct it to anyone in particular. Of course, if several clients are flipping through your material, racing ahead of you, you probably should check with the group or pick up your pace—fast!

• *Use overheads to support illustrations or particular pages in the proposal.* It can be very helpful to have an overhead to support figures or charts you are referring to in the proposal, especially if they are complex or if the group of clients exceeds 15 or 20. It can be confusing to discuss charts, graphs, etc. when everyone is working from his or her own copy rather than a common reference point, such as a big screen graph. If you use a big screen, be sure to point to the area under discussion. If you find it necessary to use a detailed graph or page of numbers in your proposal, highlight (color, underline, etc.) the key lines you will refer to in each book to assist clients following you.

• *Acknowledge errors.* If an *error* is found in your proposal, acknowledge it, say you will correct it and promise to send revised copies to the clients. But, of course, whether you are giving an introductory capabilities presentation or a final competitive sales presentation, do everything you can to *avoid* errors.

• *Don't become over reliant on your proposal.* Many top salespeople say that while they prepare (or have prepared for them) excellent proposals, there are times when they don't even use them. A prominent real estate deal maker says his group usually differentiates itself from its number one competitor by rarely taking out their proposal at all, unless the lead presenter can "see" the clients want to be walked through certain pages. As he put it, "In a big real estate deal, the client isn't interested in whether you will use a swap or LIBOR at 7 and 7/8, but rather in the success of the deal and in how many doors you can open." Another star performer says to his clients, sometimes to the dismay of junior persons who slaved to put it together, "See this proposal? Throw it away. I'm what you need to focus on because I'll be doing the work." While this may sound harsh, the point this demonstrates is that the person is more important than the proposal, and that you need to be flexible when using your materials. You need not go page by page. Nor should you necessarily cover all the pages. You can refer to or skip sections. Once you have checked, you can resume with a comment such as "Since you know . . . let's go to. . . ." The most successful salespeople don't cover every point of their proposals. They are not over-dependent on them. They are not slaves to them. They are able to free-form. They use their experience, preparation, product knowledge, client knowledge, and their group selling skills to get a discussion going. Proposals are one of their many tools.

VISUALS

As the article, "Show and Tell, with Visual Aids," *New York Times,* October 1988, pointed out, when presenters begin to show visuals "some people reach for smelling salt. . . ." But visuals can be very helpful in selling to a group if they are designed and used correctly and have a purpose, for example, with a large group to create a common point of reference, or to simplify a complex concept. You should employ them as tools to help you *communicate with* the group, not *at* it. Unfortunately, too often visuals become an obstruction to communication with the clients. Visuals are sometimes referred to as "show and tell," and it is this very expression that gives insight into what can go wrong when visuals go up: the communication becomes *one* way. Too often salespeople darken the room and begin the A to Z coverage of their visuals while clients sit back quietly. While this kind of one-way communication to a certain extent may be necessary when making a speech, your goal in selling to a group is to create give-and-take. You need to listen, show, tell, and listen.

The primary problem with using visuals in selling to a group stems from *how salespeople use them.* The main premise of this book is that to sell to a client group today you should keep the client involved. Unfortunately, interaction often diminishes when visuals appear. The darkened room, the A to Z presentation, the pre-developed script and the failure to check for questions—all create a one-way often boring, and off-the-track presentation. This "old" approach may have been appropriate when ideas were more distinguishable, clients were less sophisticated, and competitors less prevalent. I recently met with a client who was concerned about losing its last few deals. To understand what was going wrong I interviewed several of his salespeople. I asked them to describe how much interaction there was in the deals they lost. There had not been much interaction, but they had used visuals extensively. In most of these presentations they made a 30-minute slide presentation in a dark room—one-way (perhaps no-way) communication! One of the salespeople commented in retrospect, "I think everything I did during my 30 minutes contributed to our *not* getting the business." However, in the one recent deal they had won, there was a healthy amount of client interaction and the lights stayed on!

Since there can be compelling reasons to use visuals, let's look at when to use visuals, how to create good visuals, and, most importantly, how to use visuals.

WHEN TO USE VISUALS

First and foremost, decide if visuals are appropriate. Some reasons to use them include the need to

- Work with a large number of clients—20 or more.
- Simplify a complex idea, product, or system.
- Work from a central chart, graphic, etc.
- Stimulate more than one of the senses, since a picture can be worth a thousand words. Make things more interesting and memorable.
- Show the effort and time you put in.
- Create working notes for yourself.
- Contrast two ideas, systems, or products.
- Present an overview.

Ask yourself with each visual:

- Why am I using it?
- Is it tailored to my client?
- Does it just tell my story? How can I incorporate my client's objectives as I go along?
- Can I maintain interest and interaction?

CREATING VISUALS

• *Prepare* visuals in *advance.*
• *Tailor visuals* to reflect the group *to which you are presenting,* whenever possible, if not visually, at least verbally in their situation!
• Make sure *every* visual has its own *title.*
• Include *one idea* per visual.
• *Delete all articles (the, an) and other extraneous words. Use phrases, not single words,* to make a more fluid presentation.
• Use *action* verbs when possible.
• Make sure each visual includes *benefits,* not just features important to the client. Highlight and make sure the visual *scores* the point you are trying to make. *State benefits on right visual.* One investment banker making a sales presentation said, "If I were asked to put one phrase on this chart, it would be *"Save 50 basis points".*" He should have! Check that your visuals make the point you want to make. If the graph *when interpreted* shows a savings of 1.3 million dollars, *say it.* Write *SAVINGS— 1.3 million* in a balloon or a caption. You can make sure the benefit is clear and obvious without looking like a used-car dealership. Look at the visual and ask yourself, "Does it make the point I want to make?" For example, if you want to show the growth from 1984 to 1986, why begin in 1970? This just takes up space and takes away from your emphasis.
• Maintain *consistency* in bullets, capital letters (capital vs. lower case), parallel structure.
• *Design visuals horizontally.* Many people make the mistake of creating vertical visuals. Be sure to remember to use the "horizontal" direction in creating overheads and slides. The wide, not tall, layout will give you a better fit and look.
• If appropriate, *create a visual for each key concept* in the body of your presentation, but *do not overload with too many visuals.* Five good visuals are better than 20 average or poor ones.
• Limit yourself to *one or two forms of visuals.* Don't try multimedia unless you are a pro or have engaged a pro. Save that for big sales meetings, not selling to a group. Too many kinds of visuals will just confuse your clients. For example, you

can use an overhead projector and a flip chart, but it would be overkill also to use slides.

• Be sure your visuals are *readable to everyone,* including the person in the *back of the room.*

• Make visuals for any key *charts or graphs* in your proposal/ handouts to which you will refer during your presentation. It is very helpful to clients not as familiar as you with your material for *someone to point to the big screen.*

• Use *contrast.* Select different colors for visual effect and to emphasize important information. You can also use Vis-a-vis multicolored, waterbase pens to underscore, underline, add a word, or insert a number on an overhead that is on the overhead as you speak. It can be effective to illustrate the flow of a process by drawing arrows on the visual as you discuss it.

• Think of your *proposal itself* as a visual. Have a copy for each person. Apologize if you are short one copy and arrange to send more. If you are the leader, do not give up your copy; a colleague should offer hers. However, if the most senior client in the group does not have a proposal, give him or her yours; however, at the same time ask the client nearest to you if you might share his or hers. Commandeer it tactfully, and give it back afterwards!

• Use bar graphs, pie charts, etc. to help *illustrate your point. Avoid using copies of small reprints from books or computer printouts.* When it is necessary to use a page of numbers, highlight the numbers you will address in color or underlining so that clients can easily focus on them.

• *Round off numbers.* Keep it simple; 10.4 million is better than 10,411,000, which is better than 10,410,999. Your job is to streamline the numbers and make them easy to read.

• *Remember, less is more.* Highlight the key concepts you want to communicate, then decide the best way to get your point across.

• *Simply complex concepts.* Prepare visuals for complex concepts, especially to show flow or a new concept, or before and after *comparison.* A case in point is a major New York bank that introduced an international clearing product both confusing to its own bankers and its multinational customers. Over a one-year period the bank signed up no customers for this product, although it was a money-saver for the client and a money-maker for the bank. Finally the product manager did two things:

> He created a visual which contrasted the old system, in which a multinational's subsidiaries in various countries paid one another—Germany paying Italy, Italy paying France, France paying Germany, and so on to the new system in which all subsidiaries made payments to one central point, saving both time and money.
>
> He also provided a two-hour training seminar to his bankers in which he discussed the product and provided them with brochures to illustrate the new system in comparison to the old one.

As a result, the salesforce understood the benefits of the new product. They met with qualified clients to discuss their situations and demonstrate how the product might work for them. Within three months, they had four multinational clients for this system.

HOW TO USE VISUALS

- To be effective in using visuals, *assume* they put the audience to sleep. So use eye contact and your voice to maintain contact and questions (checking) to keep them involved.
- Practice. Check all machinery beforehand so that slides/overheads are upright and in focus.
- *Be prepared.* Bring your own equipment if your presentation is dependent on equipment. Carry extension cords and check on outlets, etc. *before* the presentation.
- *Keep the lights on.* Don't develop visuals that demand a dark room. Don't change the lighting of the room or you will change the environment. A dark room creates distance with clients and causes them to withdraw into themselves.
- When you show your first visual, ask if everyone in the room can see it.
- If you are using an overhead, place your first visual on the machine before your opening, so you will be ready to go.

• Keep the interaction going. *Check* if there are questions or comments after each concept is covered.

• Introduce all visuals with transition statements. Say, "This is. . . ." "Now let's look at. . . ." After each transition statement, allow yourself and your audience a quiet second to absorb the visual before you talk about it.

• Use visuals sparingly as support tools. Do not make the mistake of expecting them to sell for you.

• You can use your visuals as your notes to *trigger* your discussion, but *do not read visuals* to the audience. B-O-R-I-N-G!

• *Do not talk to or face your visuals.* Imagine the weatherman on T.V. talking to the weather map, not the audience. This may help you remember to look at your clients. It may feel awkward to keep your feet and head forward while turning your *open hand, not pointed finger,* toward the visual, but try it and you and your clients will like it.

• Don't stand so that you or your shadow blocks part or all of the image.

• Make sure the visual that is on view matches what you are talking about. *Do not leave the visual on for more than two or three minutes, unless you are directly referring to it. One visual projected on the screen can lull the group into a soporific state.* If you are going to talk about the visual for an extended time (more than five minutes), shut your machine off or insert a blackout overhead slide. (We make our own from cardboard shirt backs.) Use these framed blanks when you transit to the next point for which there is no visual. Remember, only have on the screen the visual you are discussing. This guideline applies to all visuals, so remember to turn your flip chart page to a clean page, otherwise, the group may be looking at historical background when you are discussing pricing.

• *Flick off the switch when not using the overhead to eliminate the hum of a loud motor.* You will have enough to contend with without competing with equipment noise. Flick the equipment back on when you need it.

• Only for a presentation to a *very* large group of clients should you use a retractable pointer. With a small group, do not use pointers because they are impersonal and gimmicky. It is much more inviting to gesture toward the screen with an *open hand,* not a pointed finger! Use a pointer only if you have to identify a specific line to help clients know where to look. Better yet, emphasize the line with color or print. If you use a pointer, don't play Zorro!

• Free yourself from an overhead projector by placing your pen directly on the overhead, but remember to move it as you move on. A McDonald's coffee stirrer makes an excellent place marker.

• Keep visuals on the side where you are standing (right hand, right side) to make it easy to place them on the equipment.

• Use overlays of transparencies to show contrast.

• Avoid uncovering lines as you discuss a series of points on one transparency, unless it is absolutely necessary the material not be seen. In general, this so called "progressive reveal" is gimmicky/unnecessarily secretive.

When appropriate use visuals throughout the framework of your sales presentation, especially in the agenda, body, and summary.

• The agenda—bullet the main points you will cover.

• The body—use several visuals to outline key points.

• The summary—identify key points to remember.

REHEARSING WITH VISUALS

If you are going to use visuals, rehearse—ideally in the place in which you will be presenting. If this is not possible, create a simulation. Regardless of how busy you are, the risk of not practicing with visuals is simply too high.

For example, when the president of a small regional bank made a presentation at a state conference, things went from bad to worse. As he placed his acetate overheads on the part of the table where the overhead projector was standing, they were blown to the floor by the gust of wind generated by the overhead projector. After picking up the overheads and placing them back in order (taking about three minutes), he then stacked them on the floor. Throughout his 30-minute presentation the audience was treated to deep kneebends as he stooped to the floor to put down and pick up his next overhead. Each time he changed visuals, he disappeared from view for several seconds, then popped up and presented.

Apparently the "pressure" of presenting (even though it was a small audience of about 35 people) prevented him from improvising. He could have used the side table or the folding chairs that were at his side. To make matters worse, the overheads were reproductions of computer printouts which no one in the audience could read! A trial run before the presentation and improvisation during it could have saved both him and his audience from acute embarrassment.

THE ULTIMATE VISUAL

The sales presentation demo can be the ultimate visual. Nevertheless, everyone knows a horror story about a demo. One newspaper article recounted how a telephone company lost a major opportunity when it sent its potential client to a "satisfied" user. Upon arriving, the prospect encountered a secretary who announced that she would have to leave her desk to let her boss know they had arrived because the telephones were not working *again!* Certainly in this case this "demo" did more harm than good. However, when things go well, a demonstration can boost confidence and build credibility far beyond words. It should be noted that lap-top computers are becoming the new competitive advantage as many leading companies are equipping their salespeople, technicians, and even top executives and so on with modern information technology. But this technology is only as good as the skills used to present it. Demos can be either an ace-in-the-hole or an albatross.

Some tips to help you minimize demo problems and maximize demos are:

- Rehearse and practice.
- Check all equipment before the presentation.
- For very sensitive equipment that does not travel well, invite clients to your site for the demo.
- Use a sample or dummy program rather than a live one.
- For *major* presentations, have back-up equipment with you.
- For major presentations, when possible, use two people: one to speak and one to work the equipment or program.

- Don't go through your demo A to Z. Identify the client's need/ interest and then focus on the parts the client is most interested in.
- "Hands-on" is best, so *let the client try the equipment* and participate whenever possible. Tailor the information by letting the clients plug in their own relevant information when appropriate. For example, if you are using a terminal to sell a mortgage, let your client enter (or have you key in) the price of the home they would consider, the rate, monthly budget, etc. Don't create "slave terminals" (or terminals in which information automatically appears on each client's screen) because they can have a trance-like effect on the viewing client.
- If you are using a screen with the client, create a trialogue. Be sure to maintain eye contact with your clients and don't glue your eyes to the screen. Don't become a part of the machine. Your role is to humanize it for the client. Keep eye contact. Talk to the client, check, and get feedback.
- Custom tailor your presentation; make sure the examples are relevant.
- Be thoroughly familiar with the material *before* you show it to the client.

When things go wrong:

- Don't panic.
- Call your company for help when appropriate.
- Know when to cut your losses and *reschedule*.
- Apologize and then say no more than three times—when it happens, mid-way and as you are leaving, "This is highly unusual. . . . Thank you for understanding."

When technology is introduced into the sale, the equipment becomes a new "player" in the sales picture. The classic seller team/client team becomes a seller/client/technology trio. It is important not to become so absorbed with the technology that you fail to interact with the clients.

As you prepare for your demo, involve the clients whenever appropriate with "hands-on" activities. Tailor the information itself and, when this is not possible, relate it to the clients' situation as you present it. During the demo, use your checking skills to create interaction and incorporate their information or ideas into it. For example, you could ask, "What rate shall we plug in?", and then ask, "What questions. . . ?"

TYPES OF VISUAL AIDS—PLUSES AND MINUSES

Visuals include chalkboards, flip charts, overhead projectors, slides, handouts, video productions, audio cassettes, models, demos, and samples. Each of these can be used effectively, depending on the sales situation. Yet they are a two-edged sword with both advantages and drawbacks.

Visual	Advantages	Drawbacks	Tips and Considerations
Chalkboards	No lead time needed for preparation Inexpensive Very informal Can be created on the spot Improvisation possible/spontaneous	Cannot be seen by large groups Can be messy Can be erased Unless part of a dual/sliding chalkboard, offers little flexibility when you run out of space Chalk can cause screeching noise	Write clearly, better yet, print Remember to erase when you are finished to protect confidential information/ideas Title your work Use as back-up and spontaneous resources Tailor to client
Flip Charts	Tremendous flexibility Encourages interaction with group	Cannot be seen by large groups Requires *dark,* bold markers to be legible	Use bold new markers (not pale or old ones) Make sure all clients can read it

Visual	Advantages	Drawbacks	Tips and Considerations
Flip Charts (continued)	Many presenters feel very comfortable when writing on flip chart Portable desk-top flip charts that fit in attache case are available Can be prepared ahead of time Can be developed on the spot Can be used to write down client's ideas	Easy to make errors Can be difficult to write and talk at same time Not legible if handwriting is not good Flip charts and pads can be cumbersome to carry	Use it to make note of client's ideas Tape important pages to wall to refer to during your presentation Wrap masking tape around marker so tape is handy for attaching page to wall (not on wall paper!) Prepare ahead of time Title each visual Leave one blank page at the beginning so you can cover prepared pages Impress clients and help yourself for follow-up by saving pages on which you have written client comments, unless information is confidential or proprietary to the client—client: "Of five presenters you are the only one who saved the pages!"

Visual	Advantages	Drawbacks	Tips and Considerations
Flip Charts (continued)			Use waterbased markers so you don't stain your clothes or inhale unpleasant fumes
Overhead Projectors	Transparencies are inexpensive, light-weight, easy to carry Allows presenter to keep lights on in room (therefore, maintain eye contact!) Flexible Can be prepared ahead of time Use Vis-a-vis pens, which come in many colors, to add to or highlight on the spot Can be seen by large audience Size/focus is adjustable	Dependent on having equipment in working order Potential for problems, such as not having extension cords or enough outlets If presenter turns lights off people can get bored and sleepy in dark room and lose eye contact Keep lights up! Need to know how to use open hand to point, where to stand, and not block view To write on, need special pens such as Vis-a-vis pens in multiple colors Can be noisy	*Because of noisy hum, make sure you turn off when not in use.* Turn back on as needed Use transparencies or clear acetate pages to create overheads. Get frames for each overhead for easy handling and professional appearance Make sure the overhead matches what you are talking about and don't leave it on the screen for more than a few minutes Place your pen on transparency to allow you to be free to walk about Don't tie yourself to the screen unless you are writing on it; work with the overhead

Visual	Advantages	Drawbacks	Tips and Considerations
Overhead Projectors (continued)			Use an *open* hand to gesture to screen; don't point Make sure numbers, etc. you refer to are big enough to see/easy to see/highlighted Title each visual Link features and benefits (check that there are benefits in your visual) *Use horizontal, not vertical, format for most information* Keep lights on; don't change the lighting in the room
Slides	Easy to carry Can provide outline for discussion Can be very attractive in color, design Much better for large audiences and speeches as opposed to group selling	Tend to create speaker monologue Clients can fall asleep in dark room so don't change the lighting in the room! Expensive Takes time to make without advanced technology Little flexibility Interferes with keeping eye contact	Emphasis can shift to slides, not salesperson The slides become the presenter so they had better be great! Use *phrases*, not full sentences, on the slides Do not read from slide; use info as springboard One idea per slide Title each slide

Visual	Advantages	Drawbacks	Tips and Considerations
Proposals/ Handouts	Convenient for clients since it makes it unnecessary for them to take detailed notes Shows clients you are prepared/ considerate Outlines content Can be tailored for each client	Can be a distraction if given out before you need them Avoid using boiler plate; tailor/customize	Do not distribute before you are going to use them Make sure they are client-oriented, tailored, and professionally packaged
Video Tape	Shows real effort Can be exciting, entertaining, creative Cassettes make delivery easy Can add credibility substance	Can be too slick, impersonal, cold Must be very good quality because of standards set by TV *Danger* of creating a monologue with little opportunity for give-and-take Dependent on equipment Very expensive Dark room breeds detachment. Do not change the lighting in the room!	Check equipment *beforehand* Have it in the machine ready to go *Usually show in the body; be sure to first uncover needs and interests before you show tape. Don't do product (video) dump.* *So it registers, tell group what they are going to see; bullet key ideas* and tie to needs uncovered in need check Place yourself relative to the tape—for example, "You will see X, Y and Z. My role as an account

Visual	Advantages	Drawbacks	Tips and Considerations
Video Tape (continued)			executive is to work with each of these groups to bring all these resources to you." Ask/check if all clients can *see* the video screen before you turn it on and then check for volume After the tape get feedback/ discussion/and ask if there are any questions Ideally keep sales video under 5 minutes or create three minute blocks with room for discussion in between
Demonstrations	Provides actual hands-on experience	May not work	Keep room at normal lighting Preparation is critical Create a checklist of *all* factors and criteria that are needed for an effective presentation Communicate with specialists

Visual	Advantages	Drawbacks	Tips and Considerations
Demostrations (continued)			If the demonstration is critical, bring along a second set of equipment or plan a fall-back activity
			For sensitive equipment create a "dummy" demo disk that shows what the actual program would be like, or hold demonstration at your site

IN SUMMARY

Visual aids are just that—they are designed to help you communicate your ideas to clients. If you must choose between
either creating a give-and-take with your clients *or* using slides,
etc., and making a monologue, scrap the visuals. Keep in mind
that visuals help you communicate with your clients by ampli-
fying what you have to say, not by replacing you.

TIPS FOR SELLING TO CLIENT GROUPS

This book offers countless tips, but they all really boil down to one: SELL YOUR CLIENTS, NOT YOUR PRODUCTS.

You can "sell your clients" by keeping them at the center of your group sale. *Everything* you prepare, package and present, *everything* you say about your product, your organization, yourself and your selling team, should relate *directly* to your clients' needs.

The following tips and checklists show you how to keep your selling client-centered from preparation to closing and "next steps" to success for you—and your clients.

PREPARATION TIPS

- Analyze your client. Who is on the decision-making team? What are their roles? What are their *needs?* What is the political situation? Who will attend the presentation?
- Determine your objective.
- Prepare your proposal. Check for accuracy, attractiveness.
- Select, prepare, and coordinate with your team.
- Practice.

DELIVERY TIPS

- Give *short,* personalized introductions of yourself and each team member. Use one sentence to describe each person's role. Don't go into detail on what team members will cover. Don't talk too much about your organization. What you do say should be about what your organization has done relative to your client's interests and agenda.
- Create and use notes. Do not read to clients; refer to your notes for help.
- Use and follow the framework (opening, agenda/agenda check, need check, body, summary, Q&A, close, follow-up) to create an outline.
- Personalize the sales presentation:
  Use examples relevant to the clients.
  Use company name and/or *individuals' names* in the group.
  Ask yourself, "What am I going to say that makes this sales presentation specific to *this* group?"
- Use *benefits* and tailor what you say to incorporate the client's situation, telling what's in it for the client group.
- Be yourself; be natural.
- Create a positive environment.
- Differentiate your idea/product not only inside (features and benefits), but also *outside* (you, your organization, and your client).
- Use your six critical consultative selling skills: presence, rapport, questioning, listening, positioning, checking. Remember to check and create a dialogue.
- Keep the talk/listen ratio at least 70 percent:30 percent.
  Relate to the group. Look for the friendly faces, but don't just sell to them. Include everybody!
- Defer to seniors in the group, but be respectful to juniors, too.
- Maintain eye contact with everyone. Direct comments toward individuals, but avoid putting them on the spot by calling on them.
- Observe what is going on: Are people looking at you or away from you? Do you need to change your pace, intonation, etc.?
- Be the leader of the group. Sit/stand straight. Create a feeling of confidence and control. Direct the group by making comments such as:
  "Now we will move on to. . . ."
  "Before we go to . . . , are there any questions?"
  "I will cover three points."
  "Bob, does that answer your question?"

SALES-PRESENTATION FRAMEWORK CHECKLIST

Opening

Did you:

- Introduce yourself, your team, your roles, your organization?
- Remember to answer, "What's in it for the client?"

Agenda/Agenda Check

Did you:

- Give a *bulleted* road map of the *key* ideas you will cover?
- Distribute proposal/materials?
- *Check* if your agenda meets your client's expectations?

Client Needs

Did you:

- Ask the client participants to highlight their concerns or areas for focus?
- Invite clients to ask questions throughout your presentation?

Body

Did you:

- Position and differentiate your product/ideas (features and benefits) as they related to client needs?
- Use a logical structure: client objectives, your idea, etc.
- Stay clear, accurate, client-oriented?
- Tailor your presentation?
- Maintain a 70 percent:30 percent give-and-take?
- Take into consideration the political situation and avoid offending players?
- Tell your story from your client's point of view?

Summary

Did you:

- State the key points you *want clients to walk out remembering?*
- Personalize it?

Q&A

Did you:

- Reserve sufficient time for Q&A?
- Handle the Q&A effectively?
- Provide for questions left unanswered that you need to get back to your client on?

Close

Did you:

- Express your commitment and interest in getting the business?
- Ask for business or nail down the next steps?

DELIVERY CHECKLIST

Eye Contact
Did you:
* Begin by looking at one individual client (three to five seconds)?
* Maintain eye contact with all players, even the person to your immediate right or left?

Room Setting
Did you:
* Maximize the setting? Avoid empty seats between people? Arrange the room to your advantage?

Positioning
Did you:
* Present your product/idea as it relates to the client's objectives?
* Talk about client's situation/use names, examples?
* Use client's language.
* Make presentation specific for this group.

Team
Did you:
* Hand-select, coordinate, prepare and support your team?

Body Language
Did you:
* Read the room/make adjustments?

Visuals/Materials
Did you:
* Use visual aids to help make your points?

Proposal
Did you:
* Professionally package your proposal? Was it accurate, tailored, and attractive? Easy to read? Client oriented?

Skills/Framework
Did you
* Use presence, relating, questioning, listening, positioning, checking?
* Follow the framework (opening, agenda/agenda check, need check, body, summary, Q&A, close, and follow-up?

INDEX

LINDA RICHARDSON

Linda Richardson is the President of the Richardson Company, located in Philadelphia. The company provides custom tailored sales training (sales, negotiations, sales management) to leading companies such as Morgan Stanley, NCNB, Citicorp, Swiss Bank, CoreStates, IBM Corporation, 3M Corporation, Winthrop Pharmaceuticals, The Hartford and Tiffany & Co.

Ms. Richardson is the author of five books on selling and is an internationally recognized leader in the field of sales and sales management excellence. Ms. Richardson is also an adjunct professor at the Wharton Graduate School of the University of Pennsylvania.